Equity's Whispers

DWOEEN NGAKIÉ

ISBN: 979-8-89228-831-6   (Paperback)
ISBN: 979-8-89228-832-3   (eBook)

Printed in the United States of America

Conviction Press

DEDICATION

For all the sufferings and discriminations endured—
the brightness that inspires every word I write.

TABLE OF CONTENTS

ACKNOWLEDGMENTS

To those who stayed by my side through the calm and chaos, whose unwavering faith and constant support made this journey possible. When I couldn't do it myself, your courage and faith carried me.

CHAPTER 1

Yani's apartment blinds let in a sliver of morning light, casting faint shadows across her cluttered desk. The documents before her were neatly arranged, but her thoughts drifted elsewhere. Her fingers hovered over a particular file, a case handed to her by the chief of the fraud department, who also served as deputy police chief, two months ago. Initially, it seemed to be a minor issue, just a lull in activity in a few neighborhoods. However, Yani could not shake off the unsettling feeling it gave her. The connections were too well hidden, and the details were too carefully disguised. The crucial element lay within the document she had found, which bore the police chief's signature. What did it mean? Why would he have signed it?

The sharp ring of Yani's phone cut through her drifting thoughts. She looked at her computer screen and saw Ari's name flashed on the screen, a reminder that, even though they had not spoken in days, life outside her work still existed, seeming to drift farther away from her.

"Hello?" Yani answered softly, the weight of the case already pressing on her voice.

"Yani," Ari replied, his tone warm yet slightly concerned. "How's everything? Does that mean you're still swamped with work?"

Suppressing her fatigue and irritation, Yani replied, "I'm fine. I'm just trying to sort something out. You know how it is."

"Do I?" Ari chuckled.

Then his tone shifted, more serious. "Just don't lose yourself in it, Yani. Some things are better left untouched, even if I understand that you're always trying to prove something." Before medical school, Ari had spent years consulting for internal security and emergency coordination units, relationships that never fully dissolved, thus he had already calculated the risk Yani is in.

Yani knew he was right. Still, the unease lingered, the persistent feeling that this situation involved more than just a local crime case. While she was investigating small-time traffickers, she sensed a deeper current running beneath it all.

The chief's involvement and the signed document uncovered a much larger network of corruption that could jeopardize everything Yani cared about.

"I'll be careful," she said, not certain what she meant but knowing she had to see it through.

Ari sighed in response but refrained from asking further questions. "Okay. Just keep me updated. And remember, I'm here if you need to discuss anything."

Yani understood he was correct. Still, she couldn't shake the sense that this case went far beyond a local crime. She was investigating minor traffickers, but it seemed there was much more going on. The chief's involvement and the signed document indicated a vast network of corruption that could jeopardize everything she held dear.

She was unsure if she meant it but replied, "I'll be careful." She needed to finish this. It was the only way to proceed.

After a brief moment of hesitation, Malik entered the apartment, scanning the surroundings to ensure no one was watching. He handed her a small envelope. "I was reviewing some documents, just routine. Then I found this. I'm not certain if it's significant, but you can determine that."

Yani accepted the envelope discreetly. Inside was a single sheet of paper, a report that had been recently filed. Her heart sank as she read the paragraph. She recognized the name on the report. It was the same as the one on the chief's signed form.

She asked, barely above a whisper, "Where did you find this?"

Malik expressed uncertainty about the importance of what he had just handed her. "It's just a random file from the storage room. Now that I see it, I'm not sure, but I didn't think it would be significant."

Yani's mind was already working at full capacity. Her earlier suspicion that something was amiss had been validated. She realized that this case was not a typical inquiry. She was unaware that this file was tied to a much more serious matter. "Malik," she said firmly, "you have no idea what you just gave me. The case I've been working on is connected to this file, and you need to stay now that you are involved."

Malik acknowledged with wide eyes and a nod that seemed to say he had discovered something more significant than he had anticipated.

Although many thoughts were running through her mind, Yani's voice remained steady as she said, "I need you to leave now." As she observed him walking down the short stairway, she directed him to the door, her hand resting on the edge of it. His cautious footsteps created a faint echo before fading into the tranquil sounds of the morning.

Yani took a deep breath and closed the door behind her. The situation felt increasingly burdensome. Holding onto Malik's envelope, she leaned against the door. The contents confirmed her deepest concerns. Whatever she was dealing with was deeply rooted and extensive.

Yet there was no time to waste. Action was needed, and it had to be well-planned. She hurried to her desk and retrieved the original paperwork, along with the envelope she had found two months earlier. When the pieces were compared, a more precise understanding began to form: dates, names, and transactions indicated more than just minor corruption. The document Malik had found referenced the transfer of seized assets, clearly serving as a guise for money laundering. The signatures matched.

Malik's discovery of the material was not coincidental; someone had inadvertently left a trail. However, this served as a warning. If she had noticed it, it was likely that others would recognize it as well. Yani understood that if they did, she would become their target.

She opened her desk drawer and retrieved a small unlabeled black notebook. This notebook had been in use for several months, containing her observations, notes, and collected evidence. When she added Malik's envelope to the pages, she cross-referenced the information and annotated potential connections. Keeping such a record would help her navigate the disarray, despite the inherent risks involved.

Yani glanced at the timepiece. The station seemed quieter than usual, and it was still early enough for her presence to go unnoticed. She had a small window of opportunity.

She grabbed her jacket and tucked the paperwork and notes into an inner pocket. The slight weight against her served as a constant reminder of the risk she was facing. At the door, she paused and placed her hand on the handle. For a fleeting moment, doubt crept in. Was she ready for this?

A loud knock broke her concentration.

Her heart raced as she contemplated the stillness that felt uncomfortable. The knock echoed again, louder this time. Whoever it was wasn't going away.

Yani felt her breath catch as she peered through the peephole. A figure stood outside, their face obscured by the hood of a heavy jacket. Instinctively, her hand moved to the small knife in her jacket pocket. She didn't open the door. Instead, she waited, motionless, until the footsteps outside faded.

Yani woke up early the next day. Aside from the faint sounds of the city awakening outside, her small apartment was quiet. She sat at her kitchen table with a hot cup of coffee, her notebook, and a crumpled report in front of her. The names on the paper were significant, key figures connected to various parts of the system.

She traced her fingers over the broken letters, linking them to the notes she had gathered over the past few months. The study suggested a network of kickbacks and bribery involving influential individuals and an offshore account used for laundering money. While the document provided a direction for her investigation, it was insufficient to implicate anyone.

By the time the sun rose, she had developed a plan. Yani required more information and needed it promptly. If Matamba was correct and others were starting to take notice, she had to remain proactive. She decided to meet with Jules Mavimba, a mid-level contractor who could provide insights about someone on the list. Jules was known for his role as a liaison among some of the city's prominent figures and was knowledgeable about the intricacies of the situation.

As Yani approached a small café on the edge of the commercial district, the street was quiet. Familiar with Jules' routine, she knew he frequented this café in the mornings. Upon entering, she chose a table in the corner to observe the entrance. Yani ordered tea from a waitress but had no intention of consuming it.

Her wait was brief. A few minutes later, Jules entered the café, his slim features and quick movements seemingly contrasting with his sharp suit. He took a seat at a table by the window and ordered his usual croissant and black coffee.

Yani stood up and approached him, feeling a sense of urgency.

"Jules Mavimba?" she asked in a calm yet firm voice.

Jules paused mid-motion as he raised his coffee, looking at her in surprise. "Who's asking?"

"I'm Detective Yani. I need to speak with you."

Jules narrowed his eyes as he studied her. "Detective, this isn't a good time for me."

"I believe it is," Yani replied, her expression neutral as she sat down across from him. "Jules, I am aware of the offshore accounts and the transactions."

He laughed, trying to mask the slight nervousness in his voice. "I don't know what you're talking about."

Yani leaned in slightly. "Please don't underestimate me. I found a report with your name on it. The situation is escalating for everyone involved. You could protect yourself by cooperating now."

Jules glanced around the café, appearing uneasy. "You shouldn't be here," he said. "If they see us talking,"

Yani interrupted, "Then you have even more reason to share what you know before it's too late."

He fidgeted with the edge of his coffee cup, remaining silent for a moment. Finally, he exhaled. "What do you want to know?"

"Everything," Yani stated calmly. "Who is leading this operation? Who is in charge?"

Jules hesitated before he lowered his voice. "Henda is a name you should investigate. He is responsible for organizing everything. He oversees businesspeople, police officers, and politicians. However, if you're pursuing Henda," he shook his head, "you should be cautious."

The mention of the name caused Yani's heart to race. Henda. Although she had heard rumors before, this was the first time it had been spoken directly.

She pressed on, "Where can I find him?"

Jules leaned back, his expression neutral. "That's all I can share. I would be in trouble if I said more."

Yani weighed her options as she looked at him. To avoid scaring him off, she chose not to push too hard. "All right," she said as she stood up. "But you know how to reach me if you think of anything else."

With a look of relief, Jules nodded. "Take care, Detective. You have no idea how serious this is."

The new information made Yani's thoughts race as she left the café. She recognized that Henda was the key, but she also understood Jules was right; this situation was precarious.

Time seemed to pass more quickly than usual, and the stakes had risen. A block away, her car was parked, a nondescript sedan that blended into the city's hustle. By instinct, she walked briskly, scanning her surroundings. Jules's anxious demeanor surprised her, but she knew she couldn't let fear hold her back. She had to act as if nothing had changed if anyone was watching.

By the time she reached her car, nearly twelve hours had passed since she first opened the file in her apartment. Yani closed the doors, settled into the driver's seat, and paused with her hands on the steering wheel. The city around her buzzed with honking horns, people rushing to work, and the familiar noise of everyday life. Yet nothing felt normal to her now.

With her next move already planned, she turned on the engine. While the storm raged outside, work would provide her with a temporary distraction, a facade of normalcy. She needed to convince herself that nothing was amiss and that she wasn't delving into a scheme that could jeopardize her. It was already late afternoon when her phone vibrated in the cupholder.

Her thoughts raced as she merged into traffic. She had to access the department's secure database, but logging in posed a risk of triggering alarms. This meant she needed to locate someone she could trust.

She was pulled out of her thoughts when her phone vibrated in the cupholder. A glance at the screen showed it was Matamba.

She answered the call in a steady tone. "What is it?"

Matamba replied, "I think you are being followed."

Yani's eyes moved to the rearview mirror as she tightened her grip on the steering wheel. "What are you talking about?"

"A black SUV has been parked across from your apartment all morning. It also followed you as you left the café."

Yani's heart began to race. She looked at the cars behind her and checked the mirror again. A sleek black SUV was three cars back, maintaining a steady distance.

"Don't stop driving," Matamba instructed. "Avoid going directly to work. Continue driving and see if they follow."

Yani's heart pounded, but she tried to stay calm. "I understand. I'll call you back."

She ended the call and took a side street that diverged from her usual route. Her mind was racing as she considered her options, realizing someone was aware of her movements.

As her intuition sharpened, she maneuvered through a web of side streets, adjusting her speed and navigating tight turns. She continued to move alongside the black SUV, confirming that she was being followed.

Yani clenched her jaw, determined to shake them off quietly. Spotting an alleyway ahead, she made a quick decision to turn sharply onto the narrow path. The sound of tires screeching against the asphalt echoed off the brick walls.

Taking a deep breath, Yani glanced toward the station. Although she was not yet safe, she knew she could not let fear dictate her actions. This struggle was no longer only about her; it was also about those who had been silenced, forced, or harmed by the very system she had fought against.

She drove through the alley, emerged onto another street, and blended into traffic. Checking her rearview mirror, she noticed the SUV was no longer in sight.

As Yani approached the precinct, she mentally prepared for her next steps. She needed to proceed cautiously, as the work environment was becoming increasingly complicated. Nonetheless, she felt ready for what lay ahead.

Holding the printed documents securely under her jacket, Yani exited the police chief's office, her heartbeat quickening. Each creak of the floor and the distant chatter from her coworkers heightened her anxiety, making her more alert. She understood the stakes, her actions could have serious consequences beyond just her job. However, she recognized the importance of the names on the documents.

Upon reaching the parking lot, Yani spotted her vehicle. A sense of relief washed over her as she approached it, but just as she opened the door, a voice called out to her.

"Hi there, Yani."

Looking up, she saw Ondo, a police officer from the morality department, standing near the black SUV that had followed her earlier. Despite his relaxed demeanor, his intense gaze made her uneasy.

Steadying her voice, she replied, "Hey, Ondo." With her heart racing, she gripped the car door tightly.

"I didn't see you earlier. Busy day?" Ondo asked, his tone slightly off, leaving Yani feeling uncertain.

Sliding into the driver's seat, she replied, "Yeah, catching up on paperwork. You know how it is."

Ondo offered a slight smile that didn't reach his eyes. "Obviously. Well, be careful driving." He lingered for a moment longer than necessary before returning to the SUV.

Yani closed the door with a sense of urgency. She knew there was no need to verify the SUV following her; it was already familiar. Panic began to rise, but she forced herself to drive normally as she started the engine and exited the parking lot.

After driving a few blocks, she checked the rearview mirror. The same SUV was trailing her. Her expression hardened as she reached for her phone and called Ari.

"What's wrong, Yani?" Ari asked, his voice calm but hinting at concern.

"I'm being followed," Yani replied in a measured tone. "I have a significant plan, but I'm not sure how long I can keep it up. I think they know."

"Where are you right now?" Ari asked.

"Driving." She quickly turned onto a quieter street. "The SUV from the station is behind me again."

Ari responded promptly, "You need to get off the radar. Don't go back to work or home. Can you meet me somewhere?"

Yani tightened her grip on the steering wheel. "Where?"

"Do you remember the old clinic where I worked? The one near the industrial area? It's not active anymore. I'll meet you there if you can."

Yani replied, "I got it," hung up, and focused on the road. Before heading to Ari, she needed to lose her pursuer. Taking a deep breath, she formulated her next move. Yani was well-acquainted with these streets, even if the SUV was faster.

She tried to shake her tail by making a sharp turn and navigating a series of side streets and narrow alleys. The contents of the documents she carried were worth the effort, and she was determined to continue her pursuit. Despite uncovering more corruption than she ever expected, Yani pressed on resolutely.

As she maneuvered through the city's underbelly, the sound of the engine behind her began to fade. The streets served as her guide, revealing both the presence of her allies and places to hide. With each passing moment, she felt closer to freedom, or at least to a brief respite from her pursuer.

Her tires screeched as she took the bends, and her mind raced with thoughts of Ari. She knew he wouldn't contact her unless it was urgent. But why the clinic? What did he know? The old building had been abandoned for years, left to decay amid the grime and smoke of the industrial area. If the secret held significance, it was the perfect location for a meeting, and tonight it was crucial to stay hidden.

The SUV she was evading disappeared after she took a particularly sharp turn down an alley so narrow that it brushed against her car's side mirrors. Yani exhaled, feeling a mix of tension and relief. For a brief moment, she had succeeded in evading her pursuer.

Slowing down to regain her composure, she turned onto a less congested route. Her heart raced, not with fear, but from a strong desire to reveal the truth. She could feel the edge of the envelope that Ari had advised her to protect, tucked safely in her jacket pocket. Despite its light weight, the contents had the potential to ruin lives, and maybe even save her own.

As she approached the industrial district, marked by towering smokestacks, Yani steeled herself. Just ahead was the clinic, with its broken windows reflecting the moonlight like sharp teeth. She parked her car in the shadow of an old warehouse and walked cautiously yet purposefully toward the clinic.

At the threshold of the clinic door, Yani paused. Her hand hovered near her jacket pocket, and her breath hitched. An unknown number was calling, and the phone vibrated insistently against her fingers. Despite her better judgment, she answered, her voice steady but wavering.

"Hello?"

A moment of silence followed, sending a chill down her spine. Then a low, gravelly voice came through, cold and unsettling.

"You should not take this envelope."

Each syllable of these straightforward yet significant words lingered in the air, conveying a sense of menace. Yani glanced over her shoulder at the dark empty street. Despite the absence of anyone nearby, she felt a nagging sensation that unseen eyes were watching her every move.

"Who is this?" she asked, trying to keep her voice firm.

The response came calmly, "You don't need to know that," which only deepened her unease. "Yani, turn around. Leave now while you still can."

She tightened her grip on the phone. "You don't know who you're dealing with if you think threats will intimidate me."

A low, sarcastic laugh echoed on the line. "We are well aware of your identity. You're still alive because of that knowledge. But if you continue down this path, you'll find just how quickly that can change."

Yani remained frozen in tension as the call ended before she could respond. Her pulse raced in her ears, and she stared at the phone for a moment.

The clinic loomed above her, its broken windows reflecting shards of moonlight. The package in her pocket, symbolizing the unpredictable conflict ahead, felt heavier than ever.

After taking a deep breath, Yani put her phone back in her pocket. The voice had tried to intimidate her, but she refused to let fear dictate her actions. She resolved, "I'm going to find out who's behind these criminal activities."

Yani inhaled deeply as she stepped into the darkness of the old clinic. The air was thick with dust and memories. Outside, the distant hum of machinery mingled with the faint sound of water dripping as it echoed down the hallway. Her hand instinctively brushed her holster as she surveyed the room. Although she didn't expect any trouble from Ari, being cautious was crucial in her line of work.

In one of the rear rooms, a dim light flickered. Despite the uncertainty, Yani approached it with steady breathing. The soft glow of a single desk lamp illuminated Ari's figure as she opened the door.

He said, "You made it," with urgency and relief evident in his voice. "Do you have the envelope?"

Yani held it up and nodded. "Ari, what's inside? Why am I risking everything for this?"

His eyes reflected fatigue, and he motioned for her to sit down. "The truth will soon be unveiled to you. But once you know it, there will be no turning back."

The atmosphere in the old clinic thickened with tension. Suddenly, Yani turned at the sound of a car coming to a stop sharply outside. She noticed the faint crunch of gravel beneath her feet and instinctively reached for her holster, her body tensing in anticipation.

"Are you there, Yani?" called a low, familiar voice.

A sense of relief washed over her as she saw someone enter the dimly lit corridor of the clinic, concern etched on his face. Lowering her defenses but remaining vigilant, she replied, "It's me."

They hurried into one of the back rooms where Yani detailed the call, its potential dangers, and the importance of the envelope they were protecting. Ari's expression grew serious as he listened.

Rubbing his hair in thought, he remarked, "This is worse than I anticipated. We're in deeper than I realized. If they are after you, this envelope must contain something vital. We need a secure location to regroup and plan our next steps."

Ari took out his phone and made a quick call. After a brief conversation, he faced Yani again. "I know a criminal defense attorney named David whom I trust. He can help us stay under the radar and clarify the situation. He's agreed to meet us in a safe location."

Yani nodded, her determination strengthening. "Okay, let's go. The longer we stay here, the more exposed we become."

They moved cautiously toward the clinic's exit, but upon arrival, the sound of revving engines filled the air. Yani peered through the damaged blinds and froze. A group of hooded individuals emerged from black SUVs, moving in an organized manner with their faces concealed.

"Police," she whispered, her voice strained. "Corrupt forces. They've found us."

Ari's complexion turned pale. "What are we going to do?"

Before Yani could respond, gunfire erupted, shattering the silence and the clinic's windows. They both dropped to the floor as bullets pierced the walls, creating a cloud of dust and debris in the air.

"Stay low and follow me," Yani instructed. Her training kicked in as she quickly scanned the room for another escape route. She noticed a narrow hallway at the back of the clinic and signaled for Ari to follow.

The group entered the building as the gunfire intensified. Yani led Ari through the winding hallways, her heart racing while her mind calculated each step. She found an old service door at the back of the clinic with a corroded but functional latch.

Drawing her sidearm, she said, "Cover your ears." She kicked the door open and shot the latch with precision. They ran toward the shadows of the industrial zone, plunging into the darkness.

The officers behind them realized their target had escaped. Shouts echoed into the night, accompanied by the sound of running footsteps.

Yani glanced at Ari, who struggled to keep pace. "We'll lose them in the maze of warehouses," she said firmly. "Stay alert and don't give up."

Understanding the odds were stacked against them, Yani remained determined to avoid capture; she was familiar with the city. She guided Ari deeper into the industrial area, maneuvering through a maze of crumbling buildings, abandoned machinery, and warehouses. The sounds of boots on gravel and shouting grew closer behind them.

"This way!" she called out, pulling Ari into a narrow alley between two rundown storage units. Yani relied on her instincts despite the poor light from the flickering streetlamps.

Ari's face drained of color as he gasped for air. "How long can we keep this up, Yani?"

"Long enough to get out of their sight," she replied, searching for their next move. Behind a stack of abandoned barrels, she spotted an old drainage tunnel. "Go in there."

Ari hesitated, glancing at the grimy, dark entrance. "Are you sure about this?"

With urgency in her voice, she shouted, "Do you want to live, or do you want to debate it?" She crouched and entered the tunnel without waiting for a response, motioning for Ari to follow.

The tunnel provided essential cover, but it was cramped, damp, and reeked of decay. The faint light from her phone illuminated their way as they moved cautiously.

"Yani," Ari spoke nervously, "do you think they know about David?"

Yani clenched her jaw. "It's possible. We must assume they are tracking everyone we've interacted with. David is resourceful. He will know how to stay hidden. We must reach him before they do."

As they emerged from the tunnel into a weedy lot behind an old warehouse, the noise of nearby engines made them uneasy. They took cover in the tall grass and knelt, Yani motioning for silence.

A black SUV passed on a nearby road, its headlights scanning the area. With her hand resting on her holster, Yani held her breath. The vehicle slowed, its windows too dark to reveal any occupants.

"Do you think they saw us?" Ari whispered.

Yani replied softly, "Stay still." The SUV paused briefly before it continued slowly and disappeared from her sight.

She didn't exhale until the sound of the engine faded away. "We need to get out of here. We have to keep moving."

Ari nodded, regaining his determination. "David is waiting for us. Let's go."

Yani felt a growing pressure as darkness settled around them. The enemy seemed to have endless resources and pursued them relentlessly. However, she was Yani, a police officer committed to fighting corruption. As long as she remained alive, she would not let them extinguish their hope.

Yani and Ari moved cautiously through the industrial area, careful to stay out of sight. The atmosphere was tense, and the streets were eerily quiet. Yani was focused on figuring out how to reach David's meeting spot. Each step felt risky, despite her familiarity with the city's layout.

Suddenly, Ari's phone buzzed in his pocket, surprising them both. He glanced at Yani with concern as he tried to silence it.

"Who is it?" she whispered.

Ari glanced at the screen. "David. Should I answer?"

After a moment, Yani nodded. "Keep it brief."

Ari spoke quietly. "We're on our way, David. What's happening?"

David's voice came through clearly. "The safe house has been compromised. I have a backup location. Go to the canal's old rail yard. There's a warehouse with red graffiti on the east side. I'll meet you there in twenty minutes. Stay out of sight and avoid main routes."

"I understand," Ari replied, and ended the call.

Yani nodded. "It's not far from the rail yard. Let's move."

They quickened their pace through the side streets and alleys of Owendo. Occasionally, the sound of distant motors broke the silence, heightening their tension. After a twenty-minute drive through the outskirts of Port-Gentil, they reached the rail yard. The night had deepened, and every sound felt amplified, the tall silhouettes of rusted train cars and rundown warehouses came into view.

Ari pointed out a building with faded red graffiti. "There it is."

With her hand on her holster, Yani took the lead. Faint moonlight streamed through shattered windows, illuminating the interior of the warehouse, where the doors were partially open. She entered, scanning for any signs of danger, and gestured for Ari to stay back.

The air was thick with the scent of oil and rust, and the warehouse was unusually vacant. Numerous spots could facilitate an ambush, but stacks of old containers and machinery also offered ample cover.

Yani signaled for Ari to join her, speaking softly, "Clear."

As they moved toward the center, their footsteps echoed throughout the large room. A subtle sound, resembling a creaking floorboard, suddenly halted Yani. She raised a hand to indicate Ari should remain still.

"Who's there?" she called out, her weapon drawn and her voice firm.

From the shadows, a figure stepped forward with hands raised. It was David, his face partially obscured by the dim light. He must have arrived ahead of them, cautious as always.

"Calm down, it's me," he said, his tone composed yet cautious.

Yani kept her firearm aimed but lowered it slightly. "We've been followed before. You can't take chances."

David nodded. "Understood. However, we are short on time. Let's talk."

He retrieved a tablet and scrolled through the information as they gathered in the center of the warehouse. He turned the screen toward them and said, "This is what you're dealing with."

Yani examined the data with focused eyes. It included surveillance logs, coded communications, and financial transactions, evidence linking powerful authorities to a widespread network of violence and corruption.

With resolve, Yani stated, "This is enough to take them down."

David sighed. "They are looking for you, which makes them desperate. We need to proceed carefully. I've arranged transportation for you to leave the city, but we need to be on time."

The sound of engines outside grew louder before they could respond. As headlights illuminated the warehouse windows, Yani felt a sense of dread.

"They've found us," she said.

David swore under his breath. "The storage area can serve as an alternate escape. Go!"

An amplified voice rang out from outside, shattering the silence and creating a heavy tension within the old clinic building.

"Hey! People have surrounded you. There's no way out. Send Detective Yani here with the envelope if you want to survive."

Yani's heart raced as she sensed the urgency. She looked at David and Ari, her expression focused and alert, breathing heavily. Holding the envelope felt like having a live grenade in her hand.

David stepped forward, his face serious. His voice was low but commanding as he raised a hand. "Wait."

Yani regarded him with curiosity. "What are you thinking?"

David's voice eased some of the tension. "If we run now, we won't make it far before they start shooting. But exposure is our only advantage that they can't counter."

Yani frowned. "Exposure?"

David remained quiet, focusing intently on his phone as he initiated a video call. The connection chimed softly, adding to the urgency.

The screen illuminated, revealing the faces of his sister, a journalist, and a lawyer. David's voice echoed through the old clinic building, captivating the attention of those present; some were drowsy while others were startled.

One journalist inquired with concern, "David, what's happening?"

David's expression tightened as he raised the phone, speaking loudly enough for those outside to hear. "We are currently in an old clinic building in

Port-Gentil's rail yard, surrounded by heavily armed police officers who claim to be here for justice. In truth, their aim is to silence us. We possess evidence that could potentially implicate some of the most powerful figures in our nation." He gestured toward Yani. "Furthermore, the envelope she holds contains proof of their corruption. This call serves as our witness in case anything happens to us."

The reactions among journalists and activists varied; some began recording the stream while others updated their social media platforms.

The police officers outside appeared restless. A voice amplified through a megaphone, colder and more authoritative. "This is your final warning. No one will be harmed if you surrender the envelope and the detective."

David leaned closer to the phone, his voice resonating with clarity. "For everyone watching, this illustrates their methods: coercion, violence, and threats. However, we will not submit. This is being recorded, and the world will be informed if we are harmed."

Yani's resolve strengthened, and her breath became steadier. She addressed David with a calm yet firm tone. "This is your opportunity to risk everything."

David replied, "We already crossed that line when we exposed their crimes. Now it's about applying pressure."

His words cut through the tension as he turned back to the police officers gathered outside the building. "If you want to arrest her, do it lawfully. Take it easy. You know that anything less will completely undermine your shaky credibility."

Yani could hear the officers outside whispering anxiously, their silhouettes shifting with agitation.

Finally, the megaphone crackled to life, but the voice sounded less confident. "Detective Yani, it's time to surrender. You're going to be arrested."

David leaned in closer to Yani and murmured, "They're in a tight spot. They can't let this situation escalate any further."

Yani clutched the envelope tightly, her expression unreadable, but inside, her heart raced. "I'll go if they want me to, but they need to face the truth," she said firmly.

David stayed on the line, his voice steady as Yani moved closer to the warehouse doors. "Remember, everyone is watching. Every move you make is being recorded."

As the sound of approaching boots grew louder, Yani, David, and Ari huddled in the corner of the old clinic room, their voices barely above a whisper.

David lowered his voice even more, his anxious gaze flicking to the door. "Yani, we need to hurry. They'll be here any minute."

Ari nodded, a hint of tension in his posture despite his calm demeanor. "You have to stay quiet in the cell until David arrives. Just keep your mouth shut, Yani."

Yani responded, "I'll do my best to keep them occupied for as long as I can."

Yani felt her heart race. She understood that David's plan was risky, but she felt cornered with no other options. "I can't risk it. Once I'm locked in that cell, they'll have every cop out to get me."

David locked eyes with her, placing a reassuring hand on her arm. "We know the stakes, Yani. But remember, they can't touch you right now. Everyone's watching them closely. They can't afford to mess up again after everything that's happened. To save face, they'll try to control the narrative and spin it their way. We might just have a shot if we keep quiet."

Yani swallowed hard as the unmistakable sound of boots echoed closer. As she turned to the door, her stomach twisted with fear, but she forced herself to take a deep breath. Every instinct screamed at her to fight back and not stay silent, yet she knew that David was right. The stakes were high, and one wrong move could cost them everything.

After a brief pause in the footsteps outside the door, one of the officers stepped closer to David, his expression cold and calculating. He was testing the waters, trying to see if David would slip up.

In a low, almost threatening tone, the cop asked, "You're sure everything will go smoothly if we stick to the deal, David?" His eyes narrowed, searching for any sign of deceit.

The tension was palpable as David stood his ground. "As we agreed, everything will be fine. You have my word, as long as we keep this under wraps."

After scrutinizing him for a moment, the officer gave a curt nod. "We'll see." He turned away and signaled for his two partners to come closer to the door.

With a heavy heart, the police took Yani into custody, all while countless witnesses watched the scene unfold on David's live stream. David's voice served as a constant reminder of their precarious situation.

Just before they could seize the envelope, David's words rang out again. "The envelope is still with me. You'll only be found guilty if you try to take it."

Yani walked away with her head held high, each step a quiet act of defiance. The officers handled her with a surprising amount of restraint, knowing they couldn't act recklessly in front of the public.

As she was led away, Yani shot a fiery glance back at David. This wasn't the end; it was merely the beginning of a fight that would chip away at the system, piece by piece. As the weight of the situation settled in, Yani held her breath, hoping, just hoping, that if they played their parts right and stuck to the agreement, she might just find a way out of this.

CHAPTER 2

Nearly a day later, Yani's footsteps echoed in the deafening silence as she was led into the police cell. The clinical, glaring whiteness of the walls seemed to emanate an icy coldness that seeped into her skin. The fluorescent lighting illuminated every surface, its unyielding glare revealing every detail and leaving no shadow for concealment. The room's emptiness felt oppressive, devoid of warmth or empathy, as if it had been designed to strip its occupants of any sense of protection. The only sound breaking the silence was the soft, steady drip of water from a leaking faucet. Each drop struck the sink with an almost mesmerizing precision, creating an eerie crispness against the otherwise quiet backdrop. It felt deliberate, a sneaky instrument designed to gnaw at her nerves.

Yani sat motionless on the uncomfortable seat, her breathing steady yet shallow. Tension and the unseen weight of authority pervaded the air, making it feel heavy. She understood that the chamber was meant to break her spirit, not contain her. Every element, the cold temperatures, the harsh lighting, and the constant dripping sound, was carefully designed to undermine her determination.

But Yani's eyes hardened when the droplets kept up their unrelenting rhythm. They desired her thoughts to wander and become lost in the deafening silence. However, they had misjudged her. She would bear the cold, the quiet, and the premeditated brutality. She would not allow them to prevail.

Yani's gaze slowly scanned the space, taking note of every aspect. The immaculate white surfaces of the flat, featureless walls felt more menacing than reassuring as they seemed to crowd in on her. There was only one metal bench, its edges jagged and unwelcoming, fixed to the floor. The faint hum of fluorescent light above her created a sterile, unforgiving brightness that made time seem stuck in an unending present with no warmth. The leak from the faucet persisted steadily, each drop hammering her senses, drip, drip, drip. As it bounced from the walls and was accentuated by the eerie silence, the sound appeared to get louder by the second. It constantly reminded her of her loneliness, as though taunting her with its persistence.

The air seemed dry, frigid, and strange, as if it had been deprived of life. Even her breath seemed to break the carefully regulated ambiance of the room. The faint whispers and the sporadic shuffling of footsteps from somewhere beyond the heavy steel door reminded her that she wasn't alone. But she could just as well have been in this room. It was a place created to destroy individuality and identity, replacing them with obedience and dread.

Yani adjusted her posture, the bench's cold steel biting into her skin. She refused to let her discomfort show or give the room, or those watching her, any satisfaction. She had no doubt cameras were hidden in the stark walls, scrutinizing every movement and expression with unseen eyes. They wanted her to crack, to crumble under the pressure of solitude, discomfort, and the maddening drip of the faucet.

However, Yani's determination was as icy and uncompromising as the chamber itself. She refused to give in to their demands. Instead, she gave in to a tiny, rebellious thought. *If this is their weapon, they'll quickly realize it won't be enough to shatter me.*

The faucet continued to trickle.

The cell was a purposeful creation of misery and sterility, a masterwork of psychological warfare. With an almost dizzying regularity, the immaculate, dazzling white walls stretched upward, their clean surfaces free of imperfections. They just reflected the harsh fluorescence of the ceiling light as if they were absorbing all life and warmth. Mounted in a recessed panel, the light flickered indiscernibly, just enough to cause unease without being noticed, a subtle way to make people uneasy.

Yani's throat felt coated with a metallic taste with every breath, and the air was unusually cold. It was harsh and dry, designed to strip the body of its comfort and turn every inhalation into a whisper of exhaustion. The low hum of the ventilation system, with its steady drips sounding like a metronome of anxiety, was drowned out. Each drip struck the metal basin with ruthless precision; the intensity of each sound built upon the last, amplified by the room's acoustics until it became impossible to ignore.

The floor was a polished slab of concrete, slightly roughened to discourage any attempts at repose, and it felt cold to the touch. It possessed a chilling beauty, devoid of any human traces, with no scratches or marks. In the center of the space sat a single bench, its cold metal surface as unforgiving as the chamber itself. It starkly represented the imbalance of power here, bolted to the ground and mocking any notions of freedom or escape.

The faucet, positioned slightly off-center above the small sink, leaked gradually and deliberately, revealing the intentional design flaw. Its persistent trickle served as an agent of the room's torment, an unavoidable, continuous presence in the silence.

A slight glitter of glass above the door suggested a security camera, its lens distinct yet undetectable. The weight of being observed, examined, and evaluated was in the air. Even while she was motionless, Yani sensed that every action she took was being recorded, and her silence was just one more element in an invisible experiment.

It was more than a holding cell. It was a weapon, a precisely calibrated tool for psychological damage and control. Everything was designed to deprive a person of their most vulnerable state, including the light, the air, and the constant drip of the faucet.

However, the function of the chamber became evident when Yani sat on the cold bench with her back straight and her eyes steady. It was a trap designed to entice her to comply and become hopeless. She quietly swore that no matter how icy the room's grip was, or how keen its edges were, she would not be broken as her fingers touched the harsh bench.

Approaching Yani, the policeman's face was icy and uninterested as he entered the cell. He handcuffed her wrists with a methodical efficiency. The icy metal against her flesh was a sharp reminder of her limited world.

Her footsteps echoed dully in the sterile corridor as he took her out of the suffocating chamber without a word. Silently, they made their way to a somewhat larger but equally austere chamber. Yani was motioned to sit while the officer unlocked the cuffs with a harsh click. He nodded curtly and left without saying anything or acknowledging anyone. She was briefly alone as the heavy door closed with a finality. As she paced the room, her thoughts racing with bits and pieces of the false charges

Colonne had hurled at her, she flexed her wrists, feeling the sting of the shackles.

The silence was short-lived. When the door opened two minutes later, David entered, lifting the room's burden. His warm smile extended to his eyes in a comforting contrast to their cold surroundings.

"Yani," he said in a steady, composed voice, "it's good to see you."

Yani smiled for a moment, her determination bolstered by his presence. "David," she said as she sat down, and he took the chair across from her, "they're back at it. They have concocted a fresh untruth. This time, it's about me threatening a magistrate in his office while brandishing a gun. They assert that they have witnesses prepared to provide testimony."

David's face darkened, but he maintained his composure. "I anticipated that. Their desperation is predictable. When the truth doesn't suit them, they fabricate their version. They're attempting to control the public and position themselves as the heroes, Yani, and they're not only after you."

Yani nodded, her eyes glimmering with frustration. "David, it's not just lies. It's planned. They are using public opinion as a weapon against me."

David lowered his voice to one of conspiracy as he drew closer. "I understand. However, they're going to realize that they underestimated us."

He was already thinking two moves ahead. His expression changed from one of seriousness to one of mischief. His idea was so bold and ingenious that Yani's eyes widened in shock as he leaned in and whispered something in her ear. Yani's sudden and lively laughter caused the chilly chamber to seem to melt temporarily. She put a hand over her mouth and immediately suppressed it, but her eyes were still amused. She managed to remark, "That's brilliant," in a voice just audible above a whisper.

The policeman emerged with a grim grimace as the door cracked open. With a harsh tone and a glance between them, he asked, "What's going on in here?"

David turned without flinching. He answered, "Just a lawyer reassuring his client," smoothly and steadily. "Is that a problem?"

The cop remained silent while narrowing his eyes, which were suspicious. The faint sound of his footsteps faded down the corridor as he walked back out and closed the door.

With her confidence bolstered, Yani turned to face David as the silence returned. "Let's do it," she proposed. "Let's show them what happens when they underestimate the truth."

With his elbows resting on the table, David leaned forward and examined Prosecutor Colonne's tactics with a clinical accuracy that reflected her cunning. Although he spoke calmly, there was a steely intent in his voice.

"Colonne is a master of deception," David remarked, looking directly into Yani's eyes. "Her lies are planned. They're not merely arbitrary. She chooses just enough facts to ground them, then uses them as the basis for her story. She does this by influencing both the law and public opinion. But, Yani, she's careless. Her stories reveal that the more fractures there are, the more complex they are. And I swear to you, I won't simply point out those flaws. I'll make them bigger until her whole front falls apart."

Yani nodded, firm in her belief in David. The loud metal groan of the door shattered the tense atmosphere as it swung open before she could reply. With her aide following her like a loyal shadow, Colonne stepped inside, her high heels clicking fiercely on the polished floor. The commanders-in-chief of the defense and police forces followed behind, two additional formidable men. Their eyes were calculating and cold, and their attire radiated authority. As they entered, the air grew thicker, and their stances became increasingly intimidating.

Colonne's tone was tinged with fake civility, and her grin was razor-thin. "Mr. David," she said in a falsely seductive voice, "it appears that you brought something that is ours. An envelope? If you turn it in now, we may avert some terrible outcomes."

David did not recoil. Leaning back in his chair, he met Colonne's steady stare with unwavering assurance. He remarked sardonically, "I see you've brought quite the entourage," pointing to the men behind her. "I hope they're not here to witness yet another one of your desperate attempts at intimidation."

Colonne's aide moved forward, speaking more firmly. "There is no negotiating here. You and your client will regret not turning over the envelope."

David's face remained steady as he laughed softly and spoke in a calm, measured tone. "Sorry? Are you talking about Colonne's regret over fabricating evidence in the Belo case? Or maybe it's the remorse your police chief felt after concealing his role in a smuggling operation the previous year? Or could it be your defense commander feeling guilty about transferring funds into personal accounts while the troops lacked essential supplies?"

David's revelations hung heavily in the air as the room fell silent. For a brief moment, Colonne's self-assured exterior cracked, but she quickly regained her composure.

She said, "Careful, Mr. David," in a chilly tone. "Accusations like that could land you in trouble."

David leaned forward and met her gaze. "Yes, I have taken safety measures. I've given trusted people access to every word, document, and piece of evidence I've gathered about your operations. If something were to happen to me or my client, the world would know the truth. I've made sure you won't just lose your job, but also your freedom."

Colonne softened her tone as if turning a switch while her expression darkened. "David, let's not make this worse. Let's get some consensus."

David's reaction was prompt and uncompromising. "Those who view the law as their weapon are unacceptable. Instead of negotiating with criminals in suits, I'm here to protect my client."

Colonne's smile vanished completely. She stood up tall and gestured to her group. She stated coldly, "You've made your position clear. But don't think this is over."

The commanders and her helpers trailed closely behind her as she turned and stormed out of the room. David's face was unreadable as he watched them go. He turned back to Yani as the door closed, his tone composed but determined.

"They're in a panic. That indicates that the truth is drawing nearer to us. We'll retaliate now."

CHAPTER 3

The following evening, David sat alone in his small house, watching the news on TV. The report focused on negative media coverage and announced, "Detective Yani is now facing charges for threatening the magistrate."

The anchor spoke gravely as he continued, "Based on credible witness testimony, authorities confirmed that the investigator's actions violated the law." The broadcast showed close-ups of police officers, shots of the courthouse, and a montage of Yani brandishing a gun. It was a well-crafted piece of journalism that was deliberately vague in tone, yet its impact was devastating.

The situation became even more serious when it was revealed that Yani's lawyer, David, seemed to approve of Yani's behavior rather than condemn it. Authorities alleged that David even spoke of corruption among senior officials, claiming that the alleged secret information was a tactic to discredit the government.

A panel of analysts took over the show, and one of them, a journalist known for supporting the regime, delivered a vicious attack. She said, "This isn't about justice. Destabilization is at issue here. Instead of protecting national security, people like Yani and David threaten it."

A slight smirk tugged at the corner of David's lips as he sat back in his chair. Their desperation became more apparent the more ludicrous their lies were. He grabbed his phone and dialed the newsroom number for the channel.

He spoke with the calm authority of someone with all the cards when the line connected. "This is David, the attorney you so graciously disparaged tonight. I want to talk to your news director right now."

A rush of muted voices from the other end followed a lull. After a few uncomfortable moments, a man's forceful but cautious voice finally came on the line. "I hope you recognize the delicate nature of this situation, Mr. David. How may I help you?"

David's comments became more purposeful, and his tone sharpened. "Letting me respond to these unfounded charges on your platform is a good place to start. Your audience is entitled to the truth, not this litany of falsehoods."

The director paused. "That may be…challenging. You have to realize that we have rules, and—"

David interrupted him in a low but firm voice. "Let me explain, it would be extremely inconvenient if the information I have on your channel, sponsors, and bosses leaked to other media outlets. I'll ensure this story grows much larger than you can manage, or you can let me speak."

For a brief period, the connection fell silent, and David could practically hear the director's mind shifting. The man finally let out a weary sigh. "All right. You'll get your turn to talk. However, we'll be establishing the interview's parameters."

David grinned again. "Obviously. As long as you accept my terms, I'll accept yours. I anticipate the part will air live, uncut, and without edits. We're done here if you do anything less."

The director grudgingly consented, obviously cornered. "Excellent, Mr. David. Your opportunity will present itself tomorrow evening."

David's confidence did not waver when he hung up the phone. He would make the authorities regret their underestimation tomorrow. David was prepared to use their platform against them, and the stage was set.

There was a tangible sense of excitement as David prepared for his live appearance the following evening. He gave off an image of professionalism and power by dressing neatly in a dark suit and tie. Even though the stakes were significant, his composure and careful planning remained unwavering. There was tension and interest in the television studio.

As David was led into the makeup area, producers looked at him warily and muttered to one another. His handshake was complicated but insincere, and the news director's manner was a mix of forced friendliness and barely disguised nervousness as he gave him a quick greeting.

The anchor, a well-groomed individual known for following the government's lead, approached David with a neutral expression. "Hello, Mr. David. Let's ensure everything goes smoothly because this will be a live broadcast."

David grinned, his face courteous but unreadable. "Obviously. I look forward to presenting the facts to your audience."

David sat on the set under the bright studio lights as the countdown began. The anchor, adopting a tone meant to sow public skepticism, started the segment by reciting the government's accusations against Yani and David with prepared solemnity.

"Tonight," the presenter started, "we are joined by David, Detective Yani's attorney, who has been at the center of a contentious case. You have been charged with creating false evidence and defending a criminal, Mr. David. What are your thoughts on these serious accusations?"

David leaned forward in a calm yet authoritative stance. "Thank you for having me. Let's begin with your question's premise. These so-called serious accusations are lies intended to divert attention from the real issue, the widespread corruption within the organizations making these accusations against my client and me."

The anchor blinked, somewhat taken aback by David's candor. "Are you suggesting that the authorities are lying?"

David's gaze remained fixed. "I'm saying it, not implying it. The facts contradict the accusations against Detective Yani and me, which are unsupported by any evidence. Because we have revealed facts that the government would prefer to keep secret, they are trying to suppress us." He produced a sealed envelope from his briefcase and held it up for the cameras, knowing it no longer carried the burden of being the only copy. "This contains documented proof of corruption at the highest levels, evidence they've tried to suppress," he continued, displaying it for the cameras. "Additionally, let me be clear before anyone considers stifling me."

The team became uneasy when the studio fell into darkness due to an abrupt power outage. The room filled with long, unsettling shadows as emergency lights came to life.

The anchor glared at David, who maintained his composed demeanor. Heavy boots soon reverberated down the hallway. The studio doors swung open as the distinct sound of military precision intensified. With measured authority, armed police officers and fully equipped soldiers entered the building. Their commander, a tall, calm military chief, strode forward, his uniform immaculate, a row of medals gleaming in the faint emergency lights.

The crew froze, their muttered worries muffled by the military's menacing presence. Nevertheless, David remained calm, as if the interruption were another foreseeable part of the play. The commander's tone was stern yet measured as he spoke directly to David.

"Mr. David, we are here per directive to guarantee the stability and security of this establishment. Leaving the premises right away is the wisest course of action. There is no reason to escalate the situation."

David rose gradually, his movements calm yet deliberate. He straightened his suit while keeping his eyes fixed on the commander. "Stability and safety? Commander, a noble pretense."

"However, we must not disparage each other's intelligence. This is about stifling uncomfortable realities, not about safety."

The commander's voice assumed a tone of reasonable persuasion as he calmly raised a hand. "You're a man of the law, Mr. David. You must be aware that tensions are high and that your actions, even though well-intentioned, could further destabilize an already delicate situation. A prudent attorney is mindful of when to step aside for the benefit of others."

David stepped forward and spoke with a firm and authoritative tone. "Thank you for your concern,

Commander. But let me remind you of something significant. No matter how inconvenient it is for those in authority, a lawyer's job has always been about upholding justice, especially in a republic, not backing down in the face of intimidation."

The troops shuffled uneasily, their gazes darting between their commander and David. David continued, "Speaking of responsibility, let's talk about yours. As a military leader in a republic, it is your responsibility to defend the Constitution and the rights of the populace, not to appease the whims of an unscrupulous government. Your uniform represents the confidence of the country, not the orders of those who abuse their power."

The commander's jaw tensed, but his expression was unreadable, and he said nothing. David continued in an unflinching tone, "Commander, history is cruel to people who lose sight of their mission. When soldiers put commands ahead of morality, they become oppressors rather than defenders of freedom. However, even when inconvenient, individuals who defend justice are regarded as heroes."

The room fell silent as David's comments weighed heavily on the assembled officers and troops.

The commander looked at David for a long time before speaking, evidently conflicted. "You are a strong man, Mr. David. However, this discussion is not appropriate here."

David nodded, a determined look on his face. "Maybe not. But this argument will follow me wherever I go. Commander, you cannot stifle the truth. Never, ever, not even tonight."

After a tense silence, the commander gestured to his men. "Take Mr. David out with you, with respect."

David's stance remained rigid as he moved slowly toward the exit. He paused briefly as he passed the commander, his voice forceful yet quiet. "Commander, you still have an option. Keep it in mind," David said before walking out of the studio, his exit as purposeful and powerful as his arrival.

David's phone buzzed in his pocket as he stepped out into the crisp night air. The distant rumble of military trucks created a tense backdrop, along with the whispered voices near the studio door. He noticed Ari's name flashing on the screen and answered without hesitation. "Ari," David began, his voice steady despite the night's turmoil.

"David!" Ari spoke in a worried, tense voice. "Before the power outage, I saw the broadcast. Are you alright? What on earth happened inside?"

David smiled slightly, Ari's sincere concern moving him. "I'm all right, Ari. Cutting the signal and bringing in the cavalry was their standard stunt, Nothing unexpected."

Ari exhaled in frustration. "They were going to try something, but cutting the transmission in the middle of the interview? That's low, even for them."

As he got closer to his car, David slowed his pace and looked around for anything out of the ordinary. "This is a desperate situation. Ari, they've put themselves in a difficult position. They are struggling to maintain control as their lies come to light."

Ari cautioned, "But they're dangerous when cornered. They'll do all in their power to undermine you. You're aware of that, aren't you?"

David's breath was hazy in the chilly air as he leaned on his car's roof. "I am aware, of course. That's the reason I'm being cautious. I've prepared backup plans, and the records are secure. If they believe they can keep us quiet, they are wrong."

Ari remained silent for a while before his voice grew softer. "David, you're balancing on thin ice here. Just assure me you'll be careful. Yani needs you. Hell, we all do."

Although there was still a hint of warmth, David's voice became steadier. "I won't be leaving, Ari. They may employ every tactic known to man, but they cannot destroy us if we remain wise and unified. There is still a long way to go."

"Good," Ari responded in a determined tone. "Update me. Additionally, keep in mind that you have people looking out for you." Ari couldn't see David, but he nodded.

"I understand. I will remember that. Be careful, Ari."

Ari answered just before the other line died. "You too, David."

David opened the car door, slipped inside, and put his phone back in his pocket. Despite the uncertainty of the night ahead, one thing was sure. The struggle for justice was only getting started. He inhaled deeply, turned on the engine, sped into the night, and prepared for whatever lay ahead.

With her back against the concrete wall, Yani sat in the sterile, frigid cell and stared at the dim light that crept under the door. The subtle drip-drip sound echoing in the otherwise quiet room, the chilly drips from the faucet, and the silence had all become familiar to her.

The silence was broken by the clanging sound of the unlocked heavy door. The door opened, and Prosecutor Colonne entered, accompanied by several military soldiers and two senior officers. Yani could sense the tension in the air, and their presence was unnerving. Neither David's TV appearance nor the power outage that cut off the broadcast had been communicated to her.

Colonne stepped forward with a quick click of her heels on the floor. She looked at Yani with calculating eyes and a fake sense of sympathy.

Colonne said in a smooth but sharp voice, "Detective Yani, I'm sure you've heard about your lawyer's brief appearance on the national broadcast by now."

Yani's eyes narrowed a little, but she didn't answer immediately. This was hardly the confrontation she had anticipated. Colonne went on, her voice brimming with contempt. "Your lawyer, David, is a corrupt man, working with the very people who are trying to bring this country down. He has ties to the government, and his intentions are not quite as honorable as he makes them."

Yani maintained a bland look. Her heart thumped in her chest, but she remained fearless. They were playing a game, and she knew it.

"The reality is," Colonne added, taking a step closer and speaking softly, "David is a pawn willing to sacrifice you, my dear. He is prepared to turn against you and betray you to protect himself."

The military officers behind her looked at each other, but Yani said nothing, her eyes glued to Colonne. She sensed they were trying to control her, but she wouldn't give in.

The prosecutor became nearly compelling as her voice faltered. "Yani, we're giving you an escape route. You have hindered those in positions of authority for too long. However, we can make it all go away. You are free to leave this place as a dignified lady. We want you to abandon everything and give us the envelope your lawyer has carefully concealed. We'll make you wealthy and fulfill all your dreams."

Yani's eyes narrowed as she examined them, and her lips formed a tiny, hardly noticeable smile. The proposition smacked of desperation, but it was alluring. She knew better than to be perceived as weak. She refused to allow them to buy her silence.

"Rich?" Yani's icy voice broke the silence. "Colonne, do you think I'm a fool? Do you believe I'll give you what I know in exchange for cash and your vacuous assurances?"

Colonne's meticulously crafted mask of worry briefly slipped away as her eyes sharpened. "Yani, you've been forced into a tight spot. Don't make things more complicated than they need to be."

Yani got to her feet, moving slowly but purposefully. She had had enough of their lies and threats. Her voice was steady as she shouted, "Get out. Get out of this room, and don't return. I don't care about your offers. You have miscalculated me, and I refuse to play your devious game."

The military men and commanders looked at one another, unsure how to react. Colonne's attempt at persuasion faded as her eyes darkened. Then, in a venomous voice, she spat, "You'll regret this."

Yani didn't flinch when she looked at her. "The only thing I'll regret is wasting any more of my time on people like you." She then looked away from them, indicating that the talk was over.

Her face flushed with rage, Colonne motioned for the others to follow. Without saying another word, they walked out of the room, leaving Yani again in silence as the door slammed behind them.

Her heart was racing as she inhaled, yet her thoughts were clear. She refused to give in, not now, not ever. They had attempted to shatter her, to enlist her in their corruption.

An oppressive quiet in the meeting room commanded terror and devotion. Grim-faced ministers and high-ranking bureaucrats surrounded the hefty wood table in the middle of the room. There was a serene authority about the interior minister who sat at the head. As he talked, his steely eyes looked around the room, seeking opposition. His voice was quiet but stern as he stated, "This situation has spiraled out of control. The public has become more confident because of David's television appearance. The man is a tactician and a manipulator, in addition to being a lawyer. He will destroy everything we have if we don't take serious action."

With his fists clenched on the table, the defense minister leaned forward. "David is an issue. He has shown that he's unpredictable, and he won't back down. We'll get rid of him, swiftly and irrevocably."

The justice minister lifted a hand to calm the discussion, but there was a murmur of agreement. He said, "No. Elimination is just too dangerous. David has taken action, probably disseminated information, and is ready to strike back. If he vanishes or dies too soon, the reaction will be disastrous. A cleaner solution is required."

Constantly calm, Colonne let a cunning smile slip across her lips. "We discredit him. Arrest him under pretenses, conspiracy, obstruction of justice, or anything else we can defend to the public. We make him the bad guy. His voice will be lost once his reputation is ruined."

The police chief nodded, his face inscrutable. "That is something we can manage. Our troops will advance quickly. However, we must make sure the story is flawless. We need the support of the media."

The interior minister nodded contemplatively. "Journalists are already in our pockets. They will portray David as a traitor acting against the country's interests. We'll describe him as a man prepared to threaten to benefit."

Colonne crossed her arms and leaned back. "And what about Yani?" she inquired in a contemptuous tone. "She is the source of everything. As long as she is alive, she is a symbol of resistance. If David can be deposed, she will become the next focal point."

The defense minister's expression grew gloomy. "We ought to kill her as well. Silently."

The minister of justice shook his head. "No. She is too well-known. Now everyone is watching her. Too many questions would be raised by a sudden demise. We confine her for the time being. Sow uncertainty in her head and break her spirit. The public will also lose faith in her if she falters."

The voice of the interior minister interrupted the discussion. "Enough. The choice has been made. David will be taken into custody right away.

Isolate him, frame him, and then allow the public's perception to take over. After David is neutralized, we will deal with Yani. Take care of it, Commander."

The chief of police took out his phone and made a call. He issued the command in a clear, concise voice. "Find David. Arrest him on charges of conspiracy and obstruction. No mistakes."

As he hung up, the room fell into a tense silence. The ministers' mutual resolve was evident as they exchanged contented looks. Colonne allowed herself a small, victorious smile.

"It's just a matter of time now," she declared confidently.

Somberly, the interior minister nodded. "We should make sure it is." As the discussion ended, the room gradually cleared, leaving behind a lingering sense of malice and intentionality. The room appeared to breathe a sigh of relief as the meeting ended, but the air was still heavy with unspoken anxieties and sinister motives.

With a deliberate, almost choreographed slowness, the ministers and officials rose from their seats, their masks of composure barely hiding the chaos underneath. Their figures were lengthened by the shadows created by the low overhead lighting, which made the tableau seem like it belonged in a macabre play.

The interior minister stayed at the head of the table longer than the rest, his fingertips grazing the edge of the gleaming wood as though to anchor himself. A subtle tic in his jaw revealed his internal struggle, but his face was unfathomable, a stronghold of stoicism. He grimly accepted the consequences of his choices, his thoughts already shifting to the upcoming delicate balancing act and the political ramifications. He assured himself that he was a man of necessity rather than malice. He saw this as a responsibility rather than cruelty, a compromise of values to protect the precarious power system.

Prosecutor Colonne stood with a faint but piercing smile of satisfaction. She moved slowly and deliberately, relishing the occasion as she carefully fixed her immaculate outfit. Her mind raced with plans, calculating what she would do next to guarantee her supremacy. For Colonne, the meeting was more than just a conversation. It was a battleground in which she had triumphed. Her confidence in her ability to outsmart everyone in the room was unwavering, and her eyes flickered with a cold, calculating fire. Knowing that her capacity to twist the truth was both a weapon and a shield, she took great pleasure in the drama of power.

The defense minister walked out quickly, his bulky boots clattering on the floor in rhythm with his rigid military demeanor. The perpetual frown on his scarred face was a mask of anger that barely concealed his frustration. Being a man of action rather than words, he was irritated by the meeting's bureaucratic chess game. He believed the others were cowards, too afraid to take the necessary action. Dark alternatives and direct, harsh solutions, common in his profession, swirled in his mind, but his superiors hesitated to approve them. As he walked away, he murmured a grunt of dissatisfaction directed at no one in particular.

With the quiet efficiency of someone used to working in the background, the justice minister moved. Her slender body appeared nearly insubstantial, yet her keen eyes saw everything. As though the moral significance of their discourse had not affected her in the slightest, she wore a look of detached pragmatism. Beneath her calm facade, however, was a mind that was always calculating, evaluating, and reevaluating. She was the spider in the web, skillfully constructing stories and conclusions. She saw truth as pliable, a tool that could be molded and used as necessary. Her slender smile as she walked away gave the impression that she had already guessed the outcome of this game and had planned to win.

The police chief took deliberate steps toward the door, holding his phone firmly in one hand. His eyes held a shadow of doubt, revealing his uneasiness, but his expression was unreadable. Duty held him back, and he struggled to balance his allegiance to the system with the nagging suspicion that he was involved in something gravely wrong. Compared to the other calls he had made during his career, the one he had just made felt heavier. The doubt gnawed at him like a splinter, despite his empty assurances about obeying orders. As he walked away, he looked back at the table as though he wanted to leave his guilt behind.

The chamber seemed to moan without its occupants, now gone. The deafening hush contrasted sharply with the tense exchanges and calculated words that had just filled the air. The room was crisscrossed by long, jagged shadows generated by the faint light, trapping the remaining energies of ambition and terror like bars in a cage. Alongside the intangible burden of moral compromise, there was a subtle aroma of leather and stale coffee.

The table's smooth surface reflected the faint light like a dark mirror, standing as a silent witness. The tension and malice of the people who had occupied each seat still lingered in the chairs' fabric. The chamber was more than just a place; it was a furnace where truth had been subdued and power exercised.

In its quiet, the room seemed alive, throbbing with the lingering effects of the choices made there. The mysteries of this night would remain long after its occupants had left. It was a site of intrigue and a haven for shadows.

Nature outside the sterile structure stood in sharp contrast to the icy, methodical discussions within. A deep, limitless velvet canopy, dotted with stars that blinked like faraway, discerning eyes, unfolded across the night sky. A faint crescent moon hung low, softening the edges of reality and lending the landscape an almost dreamy appearance with its silvery sheen.

Through a forest of old oaks, their twisted branches reaching heavenward like the fingers of long-forgotten giants, the wind murmured. The movement of the leaves created a gentle counterpoint to the strain within, rustling in a soft symphony. The land was dappled in a complex dance of light and dark as shadows played across it.

A creek meandered languidly through the nearby landscape, its surface glistening with reflected starlight. The gentle sound of water tumbling over stones became a quiet lullaby for the restless earth. Its banks were lined with wildflowers, their petals securely shut against the night's cool embrace, awaiting the dawn to reveal their hidden beauty.

Far away, a natural orchestra formed, a chorus of crickets and the sporadic hoot of an owl, the sounds rising and falling in time. The subtle aroma of pine and moist earth permeated the chilly air, serving as a reminder of life's tenacity despite human manipulation.

The skyscraper stood out starkly against the peaceful scene, its sharp lines and imposing presence making it feel like an intrusion. Its bright lights cast a defiant glow into the night, bleeding into the darkness around it. Yet beyond its reach, nature thrived, demonstrating its silent tenacity and unwavering permanence. Above, the stars continued their unceasing vigil, unconcerned with people's plans inside the walls below. The workings of power appeared inconsequential in their broad, quiet gaze, a transient ripple in the infinite ocean of time.

A symphony of voices from nature filled the night, blending to create a complex and eerie song that painted the dark canvas. The chorus was dominated by crickets, whose steady chirping rose and fell with the night like an old, timeless mantra. The sound never stopped, a constant undercurrent that gave the chilly air an almost hypnotic vibration. An owl hooted in the distance, its low, resonant call echoing through the trees like an unanswered inquiry. Each hoot was punctuated by pauses that seemed as purposeful as the sounds themselves, giving the bird's voice a measured and intentional quality. It was a lone sentinel watching the night with sharp, unblinking eyes, and its presence carried a strange weight.

The silence was occasionally broken by the fluttering of wings and light air whispers that suggested invisible birds navigating the night. A nightjar's melodious and melancholy song blended perfectly with the broader sonic landscape as its gentle trill rose from the undergrowth. The rustle of nearby leaves revealed a small animal, perhaps a beetle or a rat, moving carefully and precisely through the shadows. The buzzing of insects added a delicate, high-pitched layer to the nighttime orchestra. The balmy night air reverberated with the crescendos of cicadas' droning hums as they sang intermittently. Occasionally, moths struck windows or foliage, their fragile wings making faint, staccato tapping sounds against the surface before vanishing once more into the shadows.

From the piercing caw of a distant crow to the intermittent croaks of frogs hidden near unseen water, every sound contributed to the depth and complexity of the composition. Even though the world seemed tranquil, it served as a reminder to the casual observer that it was very much alive, a current of life throbbing with energy, its rhythms old and relentless. The night itself, a silent and boundless observer of the lives unfolding in its shadows, listened above all.

A witness to the world's enduring vitality, unaffected by human affairs, the natural symphony was produced by the creatures' subtle and forceful sounds. At night, the eerie quiet of nature was not a void but a presence, a deep stillness that appeared to throb with the weight of the planet's secrets. The silence held its breath, full of possibilities but unwilling to break.

The air was thick with invisible life, and every sound seemed magnified, no matter how small. An unruly breeze caused the leaves to rustle, which seemed louder than expected, as though the quiet encircled the sound, giving it shape and significance. Time appeared to slow amid the profound stillness, with each second seeming to stretch endlessly. The environment was shrouded in darkness, with shapes becoming whispers of themselves and edges growing hazy. With their black silhouettes against the velvet sky and their branches bending into emptiness, the trees stood like sentinels. They bore their silence solemnly, as if they had seen countless nights like this and emanated an ancient stillness.

Because of the night's immensity, even the stars shone more subtly. With the lightest sighs, the wind wove its way through the darkness, a soft murmur upon its arrival. It smelled of wet earth and carried the promise of things unseen. The quiet was profound but not empty. It was the quiet of observing, of waiting, of something about to happen. It held the subdued beat of the earth's breath, the soft murmur of insects too distant to see, and the subtle crackling of life. It commanded respect and prompted reflection. The hush was so deep that it was almost deafening.

Instead, it was an area weighed down by purpose, where the icy sterility of its layout aimed to eliminate any hint of coziness or uniqueness. A steady, deliberate pattern intended to unnerve filled the space with the faint echo of droplets from the dripping faucet. Here, time weighed heavily, with the stifling silence in the chamber magnifying every instant that passed.

David, in the meantime, sat in a room miles away in the peaceful seclusion of his place, a world away from the icy sterility of Yani's captivity. This place had a very different feeling, a mix of disorder and reflection, papers strewn all over a weathered oak desk with the faint scent of coffee. Despite the mess, the room had a function and reflected the man who lived there.

The room was faintly lit, with the papers before David bathed in a gentle golden glow from a solitary desk lamp. Restless energy pervaded the space, reflected by the subtle yet lively movements of shadows that extended and flickered across the walls. The walls were lined with bookshelves full of legal journals, case files, and documents, an extensive collection of information that David had accumulated while tenaciously pursuing justice.

Through the gaps in the old windows came the faint hum of the city beyond, a muted reminder of the world outside. The silence was occasionally broken by a car horn or the distant sound of voices, but David was too preoccupied to pay attention. He bent over his desk, his pen tapping repeatedly against a notepad, his forehead wrinkled in concentration. Scratches and scuffs on the wood, coffee rings that would not go away, and a pile of envelopes in one corner, some opened, some awaiting a response, were all evidence of a life spent in service. The notorious envelope Yani had given him was among them, its contents still securely hidden.

David's thoughts raced, reliving the day's events. The power outage revealed a system desperate to stifle the truth, the army's arrival, and the ministers' overt threats. Beneath his composed facade, however, was a burning desire to outsmart the powers trying to destroy him and Yani.

Pulling back the curtains, he walked across the room to the window and looked into the darkness. The city lights extended far into the distance, a glittering web of bustle and mystery. Beneath their radiance, however, lay secrets, shadows, and an increasing uneasiness that mirrored his inner conflict.

Seeing his faint reflection in the glass, David inhaled deeply. His voice was firm but tinged with defiance as he whispered to himself, "They think they've won. However, they have undervalued us."

Ari's room stood in sharp contrast to Yani's and David's. It was located in a more sedate area of the city across town. This place had a distinct, more modest vibe but was just as purposeful. It was a space of strategy and introspection, where the subtle odor of incense permeated the air and blended with the gentle rustle of papers and the sporadic tapping of fingers on a keyboard.

The minimalist style of the room's limited decoration captured Ari's essence, calm, collected, and attentive. A laptop flickered softly in the dark, and a half-full glass of water and a few stray notes sat on a small desk beside the window. The only item on the walls was a single map pinned up and marked with pins that tracked connections and movements, indicating quiet but purposeful observation of his surroundings.

Ari's room was a haven of peaceful order and precision, reflecting his line of work. His years of study and experience were evident in the well-organized shelves lining the walls, holding medical literature, journals, and other reference materials. Except for a few open books and a stethoscope hanging across one corner, the polished surface of a sturdy wooden desk against one wall was free from clutter. In contrast to the room's serene, clinical atmosphere, the desk lamp's steady, soft glow added a subtle warmth to the setting.

A solitary, spacious window overlooked a tranquil courtyard, providing a brief respite from the rigors of his job. Everything was placed correctly, and every nook and cranny was neat and organized. The room was immaculately kept. Lavender, a soothing element he added to balance the stress of his days, lingered in the air along with a subtle antiseptic scent that reminded him of his line of work.

A plain white sheet covered an examination table placed discreetly against the wall near the desk. Everything Ari needed for work was easily accessible, and medical equipment was stored in adjacent cupboards. Nevertheless, despite the room's practical use, there was a noticeable sense of peace, an unstated haven demonstrating that Ari cared for his mind and spirit just as much as he did for his patients.

Ari was more than just a doctor in this setting, despite frequently being seen wearing a white coat. Here, he became fully apparent, a man of quiet reflection and a healer who employed both his hands and mind, constantly evaluating, contemplating, and observing. This duality was mirrored in his room, clinical yet serene, well organized yet brimming with the unspoken passion of a physician carefully bearing the weight of life and death.

CHAPTER 4

The shrill ring of the doorbell disrupted David's routine just as the morning began. Nevertheless, the familiar sounds of the kitchen melted into the background during breakfast, creating a feeling of dread that swept over him. The unexpected guest took David aback. He instantly rose, frowning slightly since he knew it was not a regular knock.

Startled by the sudden visitor, David answered the door. A young man stood on the porch, his face filled with fear and resolve. The weight of his bag indicated that it held something significant.

David, not knowing who this could be, arched an eyebrow. With a cautious yet courteous tone, he asked, "May I assist you?"

The young man gave him a fleeting, tense smile as he met his eyes. With a firm tone mixed with a hint of urgency, he said, "My name is Malik." Malik, was the same man who had quietly handed Yani the envelope weeks earlier. "I...I collaborate with Yani."

David became even more suspicious. Neither did he know Malik nor had Yani ever brought him up. "With Yani?" David echoed, taking a small step back to allow the young man to enter. Though his senses warned him to be cautious, he didn't feel endangered.

As he entered the doorway, Malik nodded, feeling the weight of his bag shift. "I've been assisting her with a few things while operating covertly. I can help you with this information. She's in danger, and even though I know it's dangerous, I..." he paused, considering what to say, "I wanted to ensure you received this before it was too late."

David stared at Malik's solemn face as he shut the door behind him. He said in a neutral tone, "All right. You can describe every detail inside. Let's have a conversation."

With a brief gesture of gratitude, Malik glanced around the room before following David to the study. He painstakingly unzipped the backpack and placed it on the desk. David saw documents, files, and multiple folders labeled with details about Yani's case. His interest sparked, David inquired, "Why don't I know you? How much time have you spent assisting her?"

Malik breathed in and spoke with a lowered voice, as though disclosing something intimate and perilous. "I've been a member of a team that works in the background, watching things and getting what we can. When Yani began looking into things more, I assisted her. She has been targeted, and the situation is becoming worse. It's too much to ignore now even though I didn't want to come forward. David, you must be aware of what is going on."

David took in the seriousness of the situation and nodded. "Thank you for speaking up, Malik. However, why now? Why did you hold off on telling me this information until now?"

When Malik's eyes locked with his, the young guy briefly appeared exhausted beyond his years. "Since it's our only opportunity. They are playing Yani. If no one steps up, they will bury her, or worse. I had to make sure you had these," he added, tapping the stack of papers before David, "but I'll continue working in the background. They'll keep her safe. They will also keep you safe."

David looked at Malik's face and saw a simple resolution, no hint of dishonesty. He sighed quietly as he sat at the desk and reviewed the files, realizing he would not be fighting this battle alone. Each paper was a component of a bigger unsolved puzzle, and David felt their weight in his palms.

He turned to face Malik, standing silently next to the desk, observing him with unease. David's heartbeat quickly pulsed. His gut churned when he anticipated hearing the confirmation of his suspicions. "How long have you collaborated with Yani?"

"Long enough to know she's not the kind of person who backs down, no matter what they throw at her." Malik's gaze darted to the door momentarily, as though he was afraid of being overheard. "However, I'm not her sole ally. I'm not here to negotiate or ask for anything in exchange. If you can assist her, we can all escape this situation unscathed. I want to make sure she survives."

With his thoughts racing, David nodded slowly. The stakes were more significant than he had thought, and he now understood the nature of the game. Whatever Yani had discovered made her a target, and her life was in imminent danger. He had no idea what would happen next but was sure he would not see her get defeated.

He and Malik looked at each other. "Malik, even though I don't know you, I have faith in you. I will not allow them to silence me or destroy Yani. We must move fast. I'll ensure we use the tools you've given me to fight back."

Malik nodded in a faint, barely noticeable way. "I'll continue to operate in the background. When the time comes, you'll know where I am." He paused before the door as he turned to go. "David, exercise caution. They're observing everyone. They're also becoming desperate."

Although David nodded, he was already planning his next move. Now that he had the paperwork Malik had given him, he only had to ensure it remained secure that way. David called his sister as Malik vanished out the door to ensure his family was secure while he carried out the plan. He had also already arranged for a second lawyer, someone he trusted absolutely, in case he was removed from the case.

There was a sense of purpose now, and the room was quieter. The weight of secrets and unmade decisions seemed to pulse through the papers on the desk. David was pressed for time. Determined to finish this, he picked up his jacket, slipped the documents under his arm, and left the room. David knew staying two steps ahead was the only way to win the struggle, which had already entered its next phase.

David's steps were cautious but swift as he moved through the office hallways. Each sheet of the papers Malik had given him contained the answers they needed to continue the fight for Yani's freedom, and their weight pressed heavily at his side. He found his colleague in her office, a shrewd, seasoned attorney known for handling high-stakes litigation. As he walked in, her eyes glanced up at him, and they exchanged a look of mutual understanding before David spoke.

"These," he replied, setting the papers before her, "hold the secret. We must be prepared for everything. Examine them, make a plan, and inform me of how we might benefit from them."

His colleague didn't waste any time. She leafed through the papers, her skilled eyes reviewing each page with proficiency from years of expertise. "This is more than I anticipated. Although it is risky, it is precisely what we require. I'll get to work on the legal plan. You visit Yani."

Appreciating her professionalism, David nodded. He took one last look at the papers before leaving the office and going directly to the police station to meet Yani. When he arrived, a policeman showed him to a sterile, bleak room, the same room he had been in, where so many heated discussions had occurred. Even though Yani was already seated inside with a rigid posture, her eyes were bright to see him.

"Malik came to see me," David began, his voice low but firm. "He gave me a large, important file," he said while gesturing to show the thick stack of papers he received. "He's been working in the background, gathering intelligence while keeping you safe. But he's also put himself at risk. He wanted to ensure we had everything we needed to protect you."

Yani's eyes softened, and a hint of gratitude flickered. "Malik…" she murmured, her voice filled with warmth. "He's been a true friend, and he's still the best. But I didn't tell you about him because I didn't want him involved. I tried to carry this weight alone and take responsibility for everything. I never meant for him to be drawn into this." David nodded, understanding the depth of her loyalty and her determination. "He's already in it, Yani. But he's doing everything he can to keep you safe, even if it means putting himself in danger."

Before Yani could respond, the door opened abruptly. A policewoman stepped in, her face unreadable.

"Yani, your doctor is here," she said, her voice as impersonal as always.

Yani blinked, confused. "I didn't request a doctor..." she said, her voice trailing off in surprise. A sense of unease swept over her, and David's instincts immediately sharpened. He could feel the tension in the air, a shift that neither of them had anticipated.

Then the person who entered caught both David and Yani off guard. It was one of Yani's colleagues, wearing a calm expression, yet there was something undeniably strategic about his manner. In an instant, the pieces fell into place.

Ari was here on purpose. He had played his part in this tangled web. David's expression remained steady, but inside, his thoughts were racing. He knew Ari wasn't just a doctor, he was much more than that. At this moment, David understood that Ari's presence wasn't a coincidence. Ari had orchestrated this visit to assist in ways neither David, nor Yani, could have predicted.

Yani's gaze met David's, and in the unspoken exchange, they both understood that Ari had a plan. This was no longer just a matter of legal strategy and evidence, the game had evolved. And Ari was now a key player in what was to come.

Despite his apparent calm, Ari couldn't speak openly because of the police officer's presence. But his eyes, those piercing eyes, were sending a silent and urgent message to David and Yani. He looked to the left, scanned the room, and then stared back and forth between David and Yani, as if he were conveying some vital information that only they could understand. Then he coughed softly, as if to divert attention, before turning to the police officer and asking politely but firmly, "Could you give me a small bottle of water, please?"

It was a simple gesture, but David knew it was a signal, a way for Ari to communicate without drawing attention. As he watched closely, David received an urgent message from his office. He scanned it and turned his phone screen toward Yani to show her the news: the trial was set for tomorrow morning.

As they digested this information, Ari discreetly slipped in another critical revelation. With a subtle gesture, he leaned slightly toward David and Yani, his voice barely a whisper. "I still have contacts inside the system," he murmured. "The police officers from Section H have been ordered to arrest David. They're coming. We have to do something quickly."

David felt a shiver run down his spine. The moment of calm and strategy they had found was starting to crack under the pressure of the situation. The threats were becoming more concrete, and they had little time.

Almost instantly, the tension escalated. The policewoman returned with six other hooded officers at her back. Their silhouettes darkened the doorway as they moved into position around David, imposing an icy silence on the room.

"David, you're under arrest. Put your hands behind your back," one ordered, his voice low yet authoritative.

David slowly raised his hands, his gaze meeting Yani's, a silent decision forced between them. But before he could move any further, Yani, thinking quickly, pretended to feel unwell.

She leaned forward slightly, her face suddenly paling. "I...I don't feel well," she whispered, her eyes lowered as if unease had washed over her. Surprised by her sudden deterioration, the officers froze momentarily, their eyes turning toward her. David, acting on a protective instinct, turned toward Yani, hurrying so that this gesture would distract the officers. Even though the situation was now palpably tense, he was at her side; this was their last chance to buy time.

As the realization of what was unfolding hit them all at once, David, Ari, and Yani understood the gravity of the situation. Tomorrow's trial wasn't just about a legal battle; it was a carefully orchestrated strategy to imprison Yani under false charges, to drown her in a sea of lies, and to silence anyone who dared to expose the truth. David's impending arrest was part of that sinister plot designed to isolate and weaken their position when they needed to be strongest.

Ari quickly assessed the situation with the sharp instinct of someone who had spent years navigating the hidden networks of power. "She's my patient," he said urgently, turning to the lead officer. "I need to take her to the hospital immediately. Her condition is deteriorating, and I can't allow any further delay."

The police captain hesitated, clearly panicked by the sudden change in plans. He reached for his radio and babbled, his voice tense. "Commander, we must take her to the hospital per the doctor's request. I need permission to accompany them. Also, what about the arrest of the lawyer?" he asked, his eyes flicking toward David, who stood resolute but wary.

A few tense moments passed on the other end of the radio before the response came. "No, we won't pursue the arrest of the lawyer," the voice replied coldly. "Not here. Not tonight. We can't risk a public spectacle." The decision was swift and calculated: David's arrest would be delayed, not abandoned, while the bigger plan to control the narrative remained in motion.

Now visibly relieved by the new orders, the captain motioned for the medical team to prepare while giving the officers in charge a sharp nod. "Get her to the hospital, now." Ari, who had been watching the exchange keenly, turned to Yani with a look of quiet reassurance. "I'll make sure you're safe," he whispered as he helped her onto the stretcher. David, his mind racing, knew that the window of opportunity was closing fast, but they had to stay one step ahead, no matter the cost.

As the police medical van pulled out of the station, Yani lay on the stretcher, still playing the role of the patient, though her mind was as sharp as ever. Ari sat beside her, maintaining the guise of her private doctor. David, his thoughts chaotic but focused, followed behind in a separate vehicle. His phone buzzed incessantly with calls from his office, the lawyer he'd entrusted with Yani's case, and various others trying to stay in the loop.

The van sped through the streets, flashing lights casting a surreal glow against the darkened city. Although the hospital was only a few miles away, the journey felt like a lifetime.

When they arrived, the emergency room doors opened immediately to reveal Ari's colleagues, already prepared, thanks to arrangements he had quietly made earlier. Several of them recognized Ari immediately; his reputation preceded him. When Yani was wheeled inside, a surgical team sprang into action. One of the senior doctors briefly pulled Ari aside, speaking in hurried whispers, before Ari returned to Yani's side.

They went into a secluded corner of the emergency room, away from the bustling activity. The surgeon, a trusted ally in their plan, leaned in close and spoke in a low, measured voice. "It's working. The system is responding exactly as we anticipated. They're covering their tracks. There is too much at stake for them to back down now. But we have the leverage we need. We need to hold the line."

Ari nodded, his face calm but his eyes filled with determination. "We move quickly. Once she's stable, we start phase 2. Keep her safe. Keep her hidden. And we'll bring them all down, piece by piece."

The surgeon gave a brief nod and returned to the team, leaving Ari standing alone for a moment, staring out into the chaos of the emergency room. The battle was far from over, but for the first time, Ari felt the weight of their victory, however small, beginning to take shape. The next move was theirs, and they would stop at nothing to ensure that Yani's fight, and their own, would see the light of day.

Ari returned to Yani's side as the medical team worked to stabilize her. Though she was still pretending to be unwell, her mind was sharp, and she could hear muffled conversations around her. The hospital was hectic, but Ari stayed close, ensuring she was never left alone. Though physically exhausted, Yani could feel the strength in the plan they had set in motion.

Ari kept up his role, speaking calmly and in control with the nurses and doctors to ensure everything was in place. He stayed by Yani's side, giving her small assurances when the room quieted enough for private moments.

Meanwhile, outside the sterile walls of the hospital, David had made his way to a quiet corner, away from prying eyes. His mind raced as he pondered their next moves. The documents Malik had brought were vital, but so was everything set in motion at the hospital. He knew that the actual game was beginning. The authorities might have pulled back on arresting him, but that didn't mean the battle was over. The system they were facing was insidious, capable of shifting tactics whenever necessary.

David rechecked his phone. He received a new message from his office; the pressure was mounting. The media was already circling. They tried to control the narrative, but the truth was their weapon, and he would ensure it was unleashed. He knew Yani had to remain out of the spotlight, but the truth behind the false charges needed to come to light.

He decided to contact his colleague in the media, a trusted ally who could help turn the tide. The story had to be told, not just for Yani but also for everything she represented.

As David typed the message to his contact, Ari's voice broke through the haze of his thoughts. Ari was at Yani's side, his professional calm unwavering. He gave David a quick knowing look before stepping aside to allow the doctor to do his work. They exchanged a glance; this moment of calm would not last, but they were ready.

David's phone buzzed again, this time with a call from his lawyer. As he answered, he was met with new information about the trial. The walls were closing in, but David remained focused. They were all playing a dangerous game, but it was one they couldn't afford to lose.

Back in the emergency room, Yani's eyes flickered open briefly as she caught Ari's gaze. It was a silent exchange, but at that moment, they both knew they had to push forward, no matter what. The world's weight might have been on their shoulders, but they would carry it together.

And just as quickly as the calm had come, it was replaced with the unmistakable sense that they were being watched. Something was coming; their enemies were already preparing for their next move.

As Ari hung up the phone, his calm demeanor barely masking the sense of urgency beneath, he watched Yani, now under careful observation, her condition still precarious. Every second counted, and the plan's second stage was about to unfold. He had set the wheels in motion, and now it was up to David to lead the charge.

David immediately got to work. His mind raced as he dialed the phone lines, reaching out to several television stations, both pro-government and independent news outlets. His message was clear:

Yani, the police officer wrongfully accused by the government, was in danger. He carefully crafted his words to maximize impact; he had to be strategic. There was no room for error. Yani's health, both physical and psychological, was under the spotlight, and the authorities had no idea that this was the turning point in their carefully constructed narrative. The calls went out like ripples in a pond, and the news spread like wildfire through the city and across the airwaves. The media, once passive pawns of the regime, were now catching wind of the controversy and secrecy surrounding Yani's health. It was impossible to ignore. Questions began flooding in: What was happening to Yani? What was the state of the trial? Was David going to show up? The walls were closing in on the government, and they could feel it.

David was no fool; he knew how fragile this moment was. As the media descended on the hospital, he directed his colleague, the skilled lawyer who had taken over the defense, to join them. Her task was straightforward: make a public statement about the uncertainty surrounding Yani's health and the trial. She would speak directly to the press, but her words would be a calculated effort to keep the pressure on the government. It was a gamble that could tip the scales in their favor or provoke an even harsher response.

Meanwhile, in the halls of the government, chaos was brewing. The pressure was mounting, and the authorities scrambled to control the situation. The trial was scheduled for the next day, but the entire narrative was in flux. Yani's sudden hospitalization and David's strategic silence left key questions unanswered: Who would attend the trial? Was it going to be Yani, the woman at the center of the storm, or would her lawyer, David, be the one to face the government's wrath? The decision was looming. Without clear answers, the authorities started feeling the sting of uncertainty.

And then there was the matter of the secret documents. The documents delivered to David held robust evidence that could expose the government's corruption and systemic abuses. The government wanted them, but the pressure was mounting. The authorities knew they had to act quickly, but could they convince David to hand over the secrets? They couldn't risk it. The public's eye was now on them, and there were too many unanswered questions. The system's collapse seemed imminent, and they were desperate to avoid it.

The authorities tried to play their final card, an offer to negotiate with David and Yani to prevent the total unraveling of their plan. But they were running out of time. Every moment that passed, every unanswered question, pushed them closer to failure. The government's attempted "amicable" resolution seemed increasingly hollow, the idea of a peaceful settlement now tainted by the dark undercurrents of their corruption.

David, Ari, and Yani knew the game had changed. They had successfully shifted the momentum. The government was no longer in control; now, it was their move. Whatever happened next would define the fate of everything they had worked for.

The atmosphere outside the hospital was charged with tension and anticipation. Camera crews jostled for the best angles, reporters spoke urgently into microphones, and the hum of curiosity filled the air. Inside, the emergency room was no less abuzz, though quieter. Doctors and nurses moved efficiently, their focus unwavering despite the storm brewing beyond the walls.

A middle-aged emergency doctor stepped out to address the waiting media. His expression was calm, his voice measured. "Yani's condition is stable," he said. "There is no immediate danger to her health. We are monitoring her closely and will provide updates as necessary." The statement was brief and clinical, designed to reassure without revealing too much. As he turned to leave, the questions started flying, but the doctor didn't linger, disappearing back into the hospital with a practiced neutrality.

The press turned their attention to a woman who emerged from the crowd. Her demeanor was poised, her presence commanding. She introduced herself with a steady voice: "I am Yani's lawyer. My name is Estelle Mayaka." The name immediately caught the journalists' attention, sparking murmurs among the crowd. Estelle was known in legal circles as a sharp and principled advocate, and her reputation was one of eloquence and tenacity. The cameras swung toward her as she began to speak. "First, let me assure you that tomorrow's trial is confirmed to proceed as scheduled," she stated, her tone calm but steady. "Yani, as you know, has been falsely accused, and we will address these accusations in court. The evidence presented by the prosecution will have to withstand rigorous scrutiny."

Her words were deliberate and carefully chosen to project confidence while maintaining a cautious stance. She avoided direct attacks but left no doubt about her preparedness to dismantle the state's case. The reporters were transfixed, jotting down notes and recording her every word.

A journalist known for her close ties to the government interrupted, her voice sharp. "Ms. Mayaka, are you not concerned that your client's actions have endangered national security? Shouldn't there be accountability?"

Estelle's expression didn't waver. She turned to the journalist, her gaze steady. "As a lawyer, my responsibility is to uphold the principles of justice and ensure a fair trial for my client. And as a journalist, your responsibility is to seek the truth, not to parrot accusations that lack substantiation." Her voice carried no anger, only a calm conviction that silenced the room.

The journalist stammered, caught off guard by Estelle's straightforward response. "I...I only meant to..."

Estelle gently interrupted, her tone unyielding but professional. "Journalism is a pillar of democracy. It is not a tool for the powerful but a voice for the people. I trust you will consider that in your reporting."

The exchange left the crowd murmuring, and some reporters nodded in agreement. Estelle's composed yet firm demeanor neutralized the government-aligned journalist and shifted the mood in her favor. As the press scrambled to process her remarks, Estelle gave a measured nod, signaling the end of her impromptu statement, and turned back toward the hospital.

The scene outside was alive with analysis and speculation, but one thing was clear: Estelle had firmly established herself as a key player in the unfolding drama. Inside, the clock ticked relentlessly toward the trial, the tension thickening with every passing moment.

After Attorney Estelle's brief conference, the media's behavior shifted into a whirlwind of frenzied activity. Reporters scrambled to relay the information they had just heard, some speaking rapidly into their microphones for live broadcasts while others typed furiously on laptops balanced precariously on their laps. Camera operators adjusted their angles, capturing every fleeting moment as Estelle walked away with an air of composed confidence.

A chorus of voices rose as journalists shouted follow-up questions, desperate for further clarification or a headline-worthy soundbite. "What's Yani's exact condition?" "Do you think the trial will be fair?" "Can the government prove its case?"

Despite their urgency, Estelle didn't look back, her silence commanding more intrigue than any response could have provided.

The media's persistence was palpable. Some reporters chased after Estelle's retreating figure, microphones extended like eager hands grasping for answers. Others huddled in small groups, analyzing her statements with curiosity and skepticism, debating their implications and how to frame their coverage.

Estelle's presence was magnetic, her elegance impossible to ignore. She was a striking figure with an athletic yet refined build that spoke of discipline and poise. Her posture was immaculate, shoulders back, head held high, as if she carried the weight of her client's case with unshakable confidence.

She wore a tailored deep navy pantsuit that fit her like a second skin, accentuating her tall, statuesque frame. The jacket featured a subtle pinstripe and a single-button closure, cinching at the waist to highlight her silhouette. Beneath it, she wore a crisp white blouse with a delicate high collar, adding a touch of classic sophistication.

Her accessories were minimal but impeccably chosen, a silver wristwatch gleaming under the hospital's harsh lights and a pair of understated pearl earrings that caught the eye without overwhelming her ensemble. Her black heels were polished to perfection, their modest height adding just enough elevation to emphasize her commanding presence without sacrificing practicality.

Her hair was styled in soft waves that framed her face, the rich, dark strands contrasting beautifully with her flawless complexion. Her makeup was understated yet flawless; a subtle sweep of eyeliner accentuated her sharp, intelligent eyes while a muted rose lipstick completed the look, lending her an aura of quiet strength.

As she walked away from the media, her movements were deliberate and fluid, exuding grace and purpose. Each step was measured as though she knew every eye was on her, and indeed, they were. Estelle was not merely a lawyer; she was a force of nature, embodying elegance and authority in every aspect of her demeanor.

In the dimly lit hospital basement, the hum of fluorescent lights filled the air as Estelle walked briskly behind the emergency doctor. Her heels clicked softly against the tiled floor, muted by the sense of secrecy surrounding their descent.

The doctor glanced over his shoulder once they reached a door marked "AUTHORIZED

PERSONNEL ONLY." He opened it, gesturing for Estelle to step inside.

The room was small but well-equipped, with a modest table, two chairs, and a medical examination bed in the corner. Yani sat at the table, her posture straight but relaxed, her expression curious. The faint sound of distant hospital activity seeped through the thick walls, a constant reminder of the world above.

The doctor lingered only long enough to confirm everything was proceeding as planned. "The arrangements are secure," he murmured before leaving Estelle and Yani alone.

Estelle took a moment to assess Yani, her sharp gaze noting the calm resolve in the detective's eyes. Yani broke the silence first, her voice steady but warm. "You must be Estelle. David spoke highly of you. I wasn't expecting you to look so... commanding."

Estelle's lips curved into a faint smile, an expression that softened her otherwise stern features. "David tends to exaggerate. But I suppose I owe you some transparency." She pulled out the chair across from Yani and sat down. "He didn't tell you I was his niece?"

Yani's eyebrows shot up in surprise. "Niece?" A moment of realization passed through her expression. "He didn't. But that explains the shared sharp wit."

Estelle chuckled softly, the sound brief but genuine. "It runs in the family." Her tone shifted, becoming more serious. "David and I agreed on the strategy. I'll be the one representing you tomorrow. He trusts me to handle it. Your role is to keep up the facade for now and play the part of the patient. This gives us the leverage we need."

Yani nodded without hesitation, her confidence unwavering. "David already prepared me for this. I'll stick to the plan. No improvisation."

Satisfied, Estelle leaned back slightly, her sharp eyes never leaving Yani's face. "Good. Because tomorrow is pivotal. The prosecution will try to outmaneuver us, but they expect David. My presence will throw them off balance."

Yani smiled faintly. "They won't know what hit them. And after the trial?" "I'll be back here," Estelle assured her, standing and smoothing her tailored suit. "We'll regroup and take the next steps. For now, trust the process."

Estelle extended a hand, and Yani shook it firmly, sealing their resolve. With a final glance, Estelle left the room, her heels clicking purposefully down the hall as the door closed behind her, leaving Yani alone to prepare for what lay ahead.

The minister of justice sat rigidly in his ornate office, the heavy curtains drawn to shield him from the sun. His gaze remained fixed on the muted television screen replaying highlights of Estelle's hospital appearance. The poised and eloquent lawyer was an enigma to him, her sudden emergence throwing their carefully laid plans into disarray. She had built her reputation outside the country, beyond the reach of local influence.

He reached for his phone with a trembling hand and called the minister of the interior. "Do you know this woman, Estelle?" he asked, his voice taut with controlled frustration. The response came quickly, but it was unsatisfactory. "No idea. She's not in any of our dossiers."

The minister of defense was similarly unhelpful. "She's not a known agitator or opposition figure. Maybe someone new David has pulled in."

The justice minister's frown deepened. His next call was to the prosecutor, Colonne, and his voice was sharp. "Who is this Estelle?"

There was a pause on the other end before Colonne answered, "We were in law school together. She's brilliant, relentlessly so. Estelle doesn't take cases lightly and never attaches herself to unwinnable causes. If she's defending Yani, she sees this as an opportunity to make a statement."

Colonne's tone grew grave. "Frankly, it's better to deal with David than with her. She's dangerous; she left this legal system years ago and never returned quietly. She's methodical and has no fear of dismantling anyone, even those in power. If you ask my opinion, we should settle this before she can weaponize the trial."

The minister of justice gripped the edge of his desk tightly. "Do whatever it takes, Colonne.

Resolve this peacefully. We can't afford for this to escalate further."

The line went dead, leaving the minister in a cold sweat. He barely had time to collect his thoughts when his phone rang again. He recognized the number instantly, a call from the highest authority in the country.

"S...sir," he stammered, his voice wavering as he answered.

A deep, curt voice came through the line, each word heavy with unspoken menace. "The trial tomorrow must not include any exhibition of compromising documents. Ensure it does not happen, or you will not attend the next council of ministers. Do you understand?"

"Yes, sir," the minister whispered, his face pale.

The line disconnected. The minister leaned back in his chair, the weight of the warning sinking in. His mind raced. The stakes had escalated beyond his control. Now it was not just about Yani or David but preserving the fragile stability of the government itself. The clock was ticking, and the choices ahead felt increasingly like a narrowing corridor, each step fraught with peril.

CHAPTER 5

The night before the trial, the city hummed with a restless energy, like a river ready to surge. It was as though something fragile and hopeful had begun to stir beneath the surface after a long period of oppression. People gathered in quiet corners, homes, cafés, and public squares, whispering about the case: some debating passionately and others speaking in hushed tones. Their voices blended into a shared murmur of anticipation, the air thick with the weight of what was to come.

The atmosphere in the neighborhoods that had supported Yani was charged yet cautiously optimistic. Candles flickered in windows, small but powerful symbols of solidarity and hope. Children's laughter echoed in the streets, a gentle reminder that innocence still existed despite the shadows hanging over them. Radios and TVs buzzed with the latest updates, stoking nervous energy and excitement.

Inside a modest apartment, David's team sat together, their faces illuminated by the glow of strategy and determination. They pored over case files, discussing legal precedents, each word charged with purpose. It was a moment of focused exhilaration; every plan they made was a step closer to unearthing the truth.

Across town, ordinary citizens gathered in small groups, the mood a mixture of celebration and resistance. Music played in the background of informal rallies; the songs tinged with defiance and unity. The air was filled with speeches, poetry, and the fervent belief that justice might finally be within reach.

The mood was less hopeful yet still smug in the high offices of power. Ministers and officials toasted behind closed doors, celebrating their perceived victories. Their laughter was tinged with the false confidence of those who believed their positions were secure.

Above all, the night sky was rarely clear. The usual haze lifted to reveal bright stars, as if the heavens were watching this unfolding drama. Crickets chirped in time with the distant pulse of the city, and a soft breeze carried with it both hope and doubt.

It was a night full of contradictions, moments of joy mixed with unease, confidence tempered by fear. Yet, for many, it felt like the cusp of something monumental, a pivotal moment teetering between triumph and tragedy, ready to tip one way or the other.

The atmosphere outside David's law firm was charged with a similar undercurrent, as if nature drew attention to a moment of profound significance. It was as if the night itself echoed the words of the poem displayed at the firm's entrance:

Under the cover of a starless night,
The city shook with a quiet plight.
Echoes of whispering in scholars' dens,
Wove threads of truth with trembling pens.
From quiet hallways where knowledge hides,
To the busy streets where power rides,
The trial weighed heavily on everyone,
A climb or a fall, a judgment call.
In the shadowy rooms where brains debate,
Weight of the rule of law or power.
Philosophers talked about truth's brilliant flame,
While liars plotted to alter its name.
Under the veil of a starless night,
The city shook with a quiet plight.
The lawyer's voice echoed clearly,
Piercing the curtain of uncertainty and anxiety.
Estelle's hands were both deft and witty.
Under her mask, she upheld justice.
Above the streets, the stars stared down,
On sleepy spirits across town.
The ticking clock marked time's rapid flow,
To the dawn of trial, where the truth would be revealed.
The ministers feared what the morning would bring,
When justice dawned on the trial's day.

The hospital's shadowy corners concealed Yani's discreet exit as she slipped through an unmarked side door. She moved swiftly, her steps silent against the pavement as the night cloaked her in anonymity. Waiting by the curb was Ari, leaning against his vehicle with an air of calm vigilance. His eyes met hers, and he opened the passenger door without a word.

Silence hung between them inside the car, not from discomfort, but from the weight of unspoken emotions. The headlights cut through the dark as Ari drove through winding streets, eventually arriving at his home, a sanctuary of warmth and quiet elegance.

Ari guided Yani inside; his voice was soft but steady. "There's something I've been meaning to share with you," he said, leading her to a room filled with small, carefully curated details that reflected his inner world, artwork that spoke of yearning, books worn from his touch, and a single framed photograph of the two of them, taken long before the trials that now defined their lives.

As Yani took in the space, Ari turned to her, vulnerability breaking his usual composure. "I've kept this for years," he confessed, gesturing to the photograph. "And I've told myself the timing was never right for years. But now, I don't want to wait anymore." His voice faltered as he added, "I love you, Yani."

Yani's breath caught, her usual strength tempered by the tenderness in Ari's eyes. She stepped closer, her hand finding his. "Ari..." she began, but their emotions swallowed the words.

Ari leaned in, their foreheads touching, the closeness igniting a quiet fire. "You've carried so much alone," he murmured. "Let me share it with you."

The night unfolded in their shared vulnerability as whispered confessions and unspoken promises filled the space. Their barriers crumbled, and they allowed themselves to be unguarded and whole for the first time in an eternity.

Later, as the world outside turned relentlessly, the two lay together, a tangle of limbs and hearts. Yani rested her head on Ari's chest, listening to the steady rhythm of his heartbeat, a reminder that amid the chaos, there was still a place for love.

The fleeting night became a sanctuary, a pause in the storm. Together, they found brief solace in each other's promise.

At the same time, in David's law firm, the lawyers watched as the man emerged from the SUV parked in front of the entrance, his presence casting an imposing shadow in the dim light of the security lamps. His tailored suit strained slightly against his ample frame, and his gait was deliberate, as if every step was meant to convey authority. The glint of a polished tie pin caught the eye, and although his face was marked with age, it bore a smug confidence that suggested he was used to having his way.

The air grew tense, the hum of the SUV's idling engine punctuating the silence. David exchanged a glance with Estelle, who gave an almost imperceptible nod, her sharp eyes assessing every detail of the scene. The other lawyers stood firm, their collective presence a bulwark against whatever maneuver the visitor might attempt.

"I am the president's chief of staff," the man began, his voice smooth but laden with the weight of power. "I'm here to resolve this matter discreetly. I've been authorized to negotiate directly with Yani and David."

David took a step forward, his expression calm but unyielding. "Negotiate? That's a curious word for a man who arrives uninvited in the middle of the night," he replied, his tone edged with skepticism. "If you have something to say, you can say it here in the presence of my colleagues."

The chief of staff's lips tightened, and for a moment, he seemed to calculate his next move. "This isn't a matter for an audience," he said. "The president values discretion. Surely, you understand the delicacy of the situation."

Estelle crossed her arms, her voice cutting through the air like a blade. "Delicacy? Is that what you call it when the government uses intimidation and propaganda to silence the truth? If you think we'll allow you to twist this narrative behind closed doors, you're mistaken."

The chief of staff's composure wavered briefly, his eyes narrowing as he turned to David. "Mr. David, we're offering an opportunity for resolution.

Surely, you don't want this to spiral further out of control. Think of your client's future…and yours."

David smiled faintly, his voice steady. "My client's future lies in the hands of justice, not in the backseat of an SUV under the cover of night. If you truly wish to resolve this matter, you can present your case in court, like everyone else."

The chief of staff's jaw clenched, the tension between the two sides palpable. The resolute and unmoving lawyers stood as a united front, their presence an undeniable force against the visitor's attempts to intimidate.

Realizing he was unsuccessful, the chief of staff stepped back. "Very well," he said, his voice clipped. "But know this: your insistence on playing by the rules might not yield the outcome you expect."

With that, he turned and climbed back into the SUV, the door slamming shut with finality. The vehicles pulled away, their taillights disappearing into the night, leaving a lingering sense of unease behind.

David exhaled, glancing at his colleagues. "That was a preview of what we're up against tomorrow. Let's ensure we're ready for whatever they throw our way."

The group returned inside, the encounter galvanizing their resolve as they prepared to face the battle ahead.

Inside the office, the lawyers regrouped around the long oak table, the tension from the encounter sharpening their focus. Estelle placed her hands flat on the table, leaning forward as she addressed the group. "They're desperate," she said, her tone firm but calm. "Desperate enough to send the president's chief of staff in the dead of night. That tells us two things: one, they're not confident in their case; and two, they'll stop at nothing to manipulate the outcome."

David nodded, still standing by the window where he had watched the SUV disappear. "It's also a signal," he added, returning to face them. "They're testing our resolve. If we show any cracks now, they'll exploit them tomorrow in court."

One of the younger lawyers, Fael Doumba, spoke up. "But what do you think they were after? What could they possibly gain from speaking to Yani directly?"

"Control," Estelle answered without hesitation. "They want to isolate her, twist her words, and use her vulnerability against us. They know she's a symbol now, a beacon for truth in a corrupt system. If they can undermine her, they undermine everything we stand for."

David walked back to the table, his brow furrowed in thought. "We need to anticipate their moves. They'll use every trick in the book to discredit us and to paint Yani as a threat to national stability, especially with the trial set to be public."

Fael glanced at the pile of documents on the table, the evidence Malik had delivered earlier. "Do we reveal everything tomorrow, or do we hold back some cards for later?" Estelle exchanged a glance with David before responding. "We reveal enough to dismantle their case and show the public the truth. But we don't lay everything bare. There's power in keeping them guessing."

The room fell silent for a moment as everyone considered the strategy. Then David spoke again, his voice steady and resolute. "We prepare for a fight tonight, not just in the courtroom. We're fighting for the truth, Yani, and everyone who's suffered under this corrupt system. This isn't just about winning a case, it's about starting a movement." The gravity of his words settled over the room, each lawyer feeling the weight of their responsibility. They returned to their preparations, poring over the evidence and refining their arguments, their determination unwavering. Outside, the city was quiet, its streets cloaked in darkness. But inside the office, the light burned brightly, symbolizing hope and resilience against the shadows threatening to consume them.

The room fell silent after David's response, the gravity of the discussion deepening the tension that already hung in the air. Christina Ngabina, a veteran of countless courtroom battles, folded her arms across her chest, her gaze sharp as she considered David's perspective.

"I agree with you, David," Christina said finally, her voice steady but laced with caution. "But playing their game requires precision. Suppose we focus solely on rehabilitating Yani's reputation. In that case, we must ensure that our evidence clearly shows her innocence and their corruption…without jeopardizing her further."

Another lawyer, Carlos Mendes, nodded. "Christina's right. The court won't entertain long arguments if the judges are already compromised. We need to be concise, deliberate, and, above all, strategic. If we focus too much on attacking the power structure, they'll dismiss us as agitators. But if we carefully weave our defense with undeniable truths, we force them to reveal their hand."

Fael, the youngest in the group, leaned forward, his energy contrasting with the seasoned calm of his colleagues. "So we focus on Yani's innocence, but what if they ignore the evidence completely? What if they declare her guilty without letting us present it?"

Christina exhaled deeply, her expression somber. "That's likely, Fael. And that's why we need the public on our side. Tomorrow, the court is as much the stage as the media outside its walls. If the people see the truth, it will become harder for the government to silence it." David raised a hand, silencing the murmurs that began to ripple through the room. "Christina and Carlos are right. We tailor our strategy to expose the system's manipulation while keeping Yani at the center, an innocent officer who has become a scapegoat. Tomorrow, we're not just defending her; we're showing the public that this trial concerns more than one person. It's about justice versus corruption."

Fael, pacing silently, stopped and turned toward the group. "And what if they try to sabotage us in court, cut off our arguments, or threaten us with contempt?"

David met his gaze, his tone resolute. "Then we let them. Every overreach, every attempt to stifle the truth will only strengthen our case in the court of public opinion. But we must remain composed. No matter what they throw at us, we stay professional. Let their desperation speak for itself."

The room grew still again, the lawyers exchanging determined glances. Christina broke the silence, a rare smile softening her sharp features. "David, you've always been the bold one. Let's hope your faith in the truth outweighs their desperation."

The group returned to their preparation, the clock ticking toward dawn. Each team member felt the weight of what lay ahead, but as they worked, a sense of unity grew, a shared purpose that transcended the courtroom and resonated with the cause they were fighting for.

The office grew quiet as the last papers were shuffled into neat piles. David surveyed the room one last time, his gaze lingering on the faces of his team. Fatigue was evident in how their shoulders slumped, and their eyes grew heavy under the bright fluorescent lights. But there was something else there too, something more steadfast, a quiet determination.

He stood by the door, his hand on the handle. "It's late," David said, his voice gruff. "We've done everything we can. We need to rest if we're going to be sharp tomorrow. Get some sleep, all of you."

Christina glanced up from the case notes she'd reviewed for the hundredth time. Her brow furrowed, but she didn't argue. The last thing she needed was to be told what to do, but she was too weary to push back. She closed the file with a soft snap and rose from her chair.

"You're right," she said, her tone clipped but not dismissive. "We've worked ourselves into the ground tonight. Tomorrow, we give everything. But tonight, we rest."

Lucas, already standing and gathering his things, gave a tired nod. "I'll make sure everything's packed for the morning. There shouldn't be any loose ends."

David watched as they gathered their belongings, moving slowly but with purpose. The tension that had filled the room for hours began to dissipate, but it didn't vanish completely. It lingered in the air, heavy and unspoken.

As they exited the office, David turned off the lights individually. The hum of the fluorescent bulbs faded to silence, leaving only the faint sound of distant traffic outside. He was the last to leave. The weight of the night pressed down on him, and he lingered for a moment by the doorway. His fingers grazed the edge of his coat hanging on the back of a chair. Everything they'd worked for and sacrificed came down to tomorrow in this fragile moment.

The door clicked shut behind him. The parking lot was eerily quiet, save for the hum of Estelle's idling car. The city skyline loomed in the distance, its lights blinking in the cool night air, but everything felt distant, frozen, as if time was waiting for tomorrow to arrive.

Estelle sat in the driver's seat, hands clenched around the steering wheel. Her mind was a whirlwind, caught between the magnitude of the case and the exhaustion creeping through her bones. She'd spent hours going over every detail, revisiting every strategy, and still, it felt like there was something she might have missed.

They would stand in court tomorrow, facing off against the opposition and their high-powered legal team. And though Estelle had won countless battles in the courtroom before, something about this case felt different. More personal. More dangerous. The stakes had never been higher.

She ran a hand through her hair, her eyes closing briefly. The stillness of the night seemed to pull her deeper into her thoughts.

Then a knock on the window. Startled, Estelle's eyes shot open. She hadn't noticed anyone approaching, and for a moment, her body tensed, ready to defend herself against an interruption. But when she looked up, she saw Christina standing there, her figure cast in the dim light of the parking lot, her breath visible in the cold air.

Christina was always the levelheaded one, the rock in the storm of late-night strategy meetings.

Estelle rolled the window down, letting in the chill. "Everything okay?" Christina's voice cut through the silence, her tone gentle but purposeful. "I just wanted to make sure you were doing all right."

Estelle blinked, taken aback by the question. "I'm fine," she said, trying to mask the fatigue in her voice. "Just...thinking. A lot to prepare for tomorrow."

Christina stepped closer, her face serious but not without warmth. "I get it. It's been a long night. But we've all been through this. You've got this, Estelle. We've all worked hard for this moment. We'll handle whatever comes tomorrow."

Estelle let out a breath she hadn't realized she was holding. "I just...I don't know. In this case, it's different. There's so much at stake here."

Christina nodded slowly, understanding more than Estelle expected. "I know. But you're not carrying it alone. We're a team. You've got the experience, the knowledge, and the drive. You're more than ready."

There was a long pause between them, and for a moment, Estelle almost let herself believe it. She looked at Christina, her colleague, her ally, and saw not just the woman who had helped strategize every move in this case but someone who truly understood the weight of the pressure they were under.

"Thanks, Christina," Estelle said quietly, her voice softened by the quiet reassurance. "I needed to hear that."

Christina smiled faintly. "Anytime. We'll face it together. Just make sure you get some rest tonight. We can't afford to be tired tomorrow."

Estelle offered a small smile in return, feeling a flicker of warmth in her chest. "I'll try," she said, though the weight of tomorrow still lingered.

Christina nodded in agreement before returning to her car, her footsteps echoing softly against the asphalt.

As Estelle watched her go, the darkness of the parking lot became less oppressive. It wasn't just about the case anymore; it was about their support for one another and the strength in their shared purpose.

With a sigh, Estelle started the car, the engine rumbling to life. She still had a long night ahead of her, but now there was a tiny sliver of calm amid the chaos. She wasn't facing tomorrow alone.

The engine hummed steadily as Estelle drove through the quiet streets, and the low hum of the tires on the road was the only sound. Usually bustling with life, the city seemed to be holding its breath. The weight of the trial still pressed on her, but she needed something to take her mind off the relentless swirl of thoughts.

Her hand reached for the car's stereo, flicking through the radio stations before she landed on a familiar tune, a song that had always calmed her, no matter the chaos around her.

"Didi, sui, Kami…" The song's opening notes by the Gabonese diva, Patience Dabany, filled the car. The soulful rhythm, rich with warmth and rhythm, wrapped around her like a blanket. She closed her eyes briefly, letting the smooth melody flow through her, feeling the weight in her chest loosen just a little.

The stress, anxiety, and pressure all seemed to dissipate for a few minutes, replaced by the soothing cadence of the music. Her fingers lightly tapped against the steering wheel, the beat syncing with the gentle rhythm of the road. The night felt quieter now, less oppressive. The hum of the engine, the melody, and the city's familiar streets seemed to blend into a peaceful moment she desperately needed.

By the time she turned onto her street, the tightness in her shoulders had eased, and her mind was a little clearer. Estelle parked in her driveway and sat for a moment, the final notes of the song trailing off. She didn't rush to leave the car; she just sat in the stillness for a moment longer.

She knew tomorrow would bring new challenges and tensions, but tonight, she could breathe.

The house was quiet when Estelle stepped inside, the familiar scents of her home wrapping around her like a gentle embrace. The lights were dim, and the calm of her space felt worlds away from the tension of the office.

She quickly changed into something comfortable, a loose robe that felt soft against her skin. The shower water hit her like a small cleansing ritual, washing away the tension from her body. As she let the warm stream flow over her, she felt the knots in her neck and shoulders begin to loosen, and for the first time in hours, her mind felt almost…still.

When she stepped out, the air was crisp and cool on her damp skin. She dressed quickly, making her way to the kitchen. The quiet hum of the refrigerator was the only sound as she prepped a simple salad, greens, tomatoes, a sprinkle of feta, and a drizzle of olive oil. It wasn't much, but it was enough to feel like she was taking care of herself. She ate in silence, the quiet of the evening settling around her. It was a humble, quiet dinner, but it was grounding, reminding her that no matter what happened tomorrow, she still had moments like these, small, fleeting moments of peace.

Afterward, she quickly washed the dishes, wiped down the counter, and took one last look at the kitchen before heading to bed. The house was still and dark now, save for the soft glow of the bedside lamp.

Estelle slipped beneath the covers, her body sinking into the soft sheets. She closed her eyes, the day's weight lifting as her mind settled into the stillness. She didn't know what tomorrow would bring, but for tonight, she could rest.

Estelle's home was a quiet retreat, with soft, indirect lighting spilling from the lamps around the room. The faint smell of lavender lingered in the air, a calming scent that helped her unwind after the intensity of the day. The living room was modest but cozy, with plush cushions scattered on the couch and a few framed photos on the walls, nothing flashy, just things that made her feel grounded.

Though small, her kitchen was neat and functional, and the refrigerator's hum was the only sound in the otherwise tranquil space. A half-drunk glass of wine sat on the counter, untouched now, as she moved around the room in a comfortable silence. The soft murmur of the radio in the background was barely audible, playing some jazz station she had put on to fill the space. The soothing notes of saxophones and smooth piano keys filled the room, the night stretching out before her in a slow, almost meditative rhythm.

The faint moonlight through the kitchen window cast soft shadows across the room. Estelle leaned against the counter momentarily, eyes closed, letting the quiet seep into her bones. The weight of tomorrow loomed, but tonight, there was only the calm of her space, the peace that came with the gentle rituals of her evening. The only sound was her steady breathing as she prepared to drift off to sleep, knowing the coming day would demand every ounce of focus and energy she could muster.

David's apartment was a quiet refuge from the world outside. The city's noise seemed distant here, muffled by the thick curtains he'd drawn across the windows. A single lamp in the corner of the room cast a warm, amber glow that softened the edges of the sparse, minimalist space. The air smelled faintly of wood and something calming, maybe cedar, maybe just the scent of a long day fading away.

He had left the door to the balcony open just a crack, the cool night breeze coming in like a breath of fresh air. It carried the faint sounds of the city, distant conversations, the occasional car passing, but they felt far away. In the solitude, David rested in his armchair, his chest rising and falling with each deep breath. The trial still occupied his thoughts, but there was a quiet peace in the simple rhythm of the moment.

On the coffee table, David's phone buzzed intermittently, but he ignored it. He had no interest in any more messages or calls tonight. Instead, he took a slow sip from his glass, savoring the last bottle of red wine. The weight of the day's decisions was heavy, but the stillness of the night allowed him to release it, even if only for a while.

Outside, the city lights twinkled like distant stars, and the air, tinged with the coolness of autumn, softly reminded David of the quiet night that had enveloped him. David closed his eyes for a moment, the steady sound of his breathing mixing with the rhythm of the night. Tomorrow would come with its challenges, but for now, he could rest.

Fael's apartment was small but full of life, a cozy bohemian space that felt like a haven from the world. The faint scent of incense lingered in the air, mingling with the earthy aroma of plants in every corner of the room. Soft, warm lighting bathed the room, giving everything a golden glow, and the low hum of a record player played some soulful music, something that blended jazz with a hint of rhythm and blues.

The windows were cracked open, and the soft night breeze swept through the room, carrying the crisp scent of autumn leaves. A mug of herbal tea sat on the coffee table beside an open book that Fael had barely gotten through. His mind wandered between the words on the page and the quiet hum of the music. He was the kind of person who thrived in moments like this, when the world outside faded away and only the present moment remained.

Outside, the rustling of trees echoed through the stillness, and every so often, a lone car would pass by, its headlights briefly illuminating the space before fading back into the night. Fael didn't mind the silence. He welcomed it, almost needed it after the day's emotional and mental toll. The soft flicker of candlelight filled the room with an amber glow, casting long shadows that danced against the walls as he let the calm of the night seep into his thoughts, allowing himself a moment to rest before the storm of tomorrow.

Ari's home was a sanctuary of warmth and softness, where the world's weight seemed to vanish, a nice place for a doctor. The soft glow of dimmed lights spilled from the kitchen and the living room, and the faint scent of lavender and fresh herbs lingered in the air from the dinner he shared with Yani. The home felt lived-in, cozy, a space he had carefully curated to reflect his medical area. A plush rug covered the wooden floor, and the couches were piled with soft throw pillows in neutral tones, creating an inviting atmosphere.

Outside, the night was calm, the sounds of the city softened by the thick curtains drawn across the windows. A few candles flickered on the coffee table, their gentle light dancing in the stillness of the night.

Yani sat by the window, staring out at the quiet street, the occasional cars passing by, but mostly, it was just silence. Ari was curled up on the couch, a book in hand, the quiet rustle of pages the only sound in the room.

Their shared space felt full of connection, a grounding quiet that wrapped around them like a warm blanket. Tonight, there was a quiet, unspoken understanding between them, an acknowledgment of what lay ahead but also of the importance of this moment, of the peace they shared in the stillness of the home. For now, the world outside could wait. Tonight, they had each other.

Yani's apartment was usually filled with life and movement, but tonight, it sat with the stillness of the night. The faint hum of the city outside filtered through the windows, but inside, the place felt empty, almost abandoned, as though the walls held their breath in anticipation of her return.

The lights were dimmed, casting long shadows across the room, but it wasn't the typical cozy ambiance. Everything felt unnerving without her presence, the low murmur of her voice, the clinking of dishes as she prepared something quick to eat, and the music softly playing in the background. The usually vibrant apartment, with its eclectic mix of colors, plants, and art, seemed almost muted in the silence.

Her record player, which often spun new soul or African rhythms, sat silently by the window, its needle resting still in its holder. The shelves, usually overflowing with books and trinkets from her travels, seemed strangely lifeless now, as if they were waiting for the energy she brought to return. A few of her favorite books lay scattered across the coffee table, their pages slightly curled from when she had picked them up and put them back down. The soft cushions on the couch, usually in disarray from her quick rests and spontaneous naps, sat neatly in place, almost too neat for comfort.

The smell of her last cup of tea lingered in the air, a subtle trace of lavender and chamomile still clinging to the room's edges, but it was fading. The kitchen, which would typically have the comforting warmth of a half-finished dinner or the aroma of a freshly brewed pot of coffee, was still. Her mug sat empty on the counter, abandoned as if she had just left moments ago.

Outside the window, the streetlights flickered lazily in the night. The wind blew gently, moving the thin curtains just enough to break; otherwise, the apartment felt quiet, as if the walls were holding onto the echoes of her laughter and conversation, which now seemed absent in the silence.

The bed was neatly made in the bedroom, but the space felt hollow. The clothes that Yani usually left strewn across the floor and the shoes kicked off at odd angles were absent. The room, typically filled with the soft sound of her music or the quiet rhythm of her evening routines, sat untouched, with only the faint scent of her perfume lingering in the air, a reminder of her presence now gone.

For the night, Yani's home was simply a place, the place she usually filled with her vibrant energy and warmth. But without her, it felt like a shell, a space waiting to be alive again. It was too quiet, too still, as if the very soul of the place was on pause, waiting for her return to fill it with life once more.

The night unfolded like a velvet tapestry, dark and rich, stretching infinitely across the heavens. The moon, a luminous pearl, hung suspended in the sky, casting a gentle silver glow that kissed the earth below. Its light rippled across the world's surface like the quiet pulse of an ancient heart, beating in sync with the slow, rhythmic dance of the stars. They glittered in the vast blackness, distant but never still, an eternal array of shimmering gems scattered like the dreams of forgotten gods.

In the farthest reaches of the sky, where the human eye cannot see, nebulae bloom like petals, great clouds of gas and dust swirling in luminous hues of violet, blue, and pink. They are soft and glowing, resembling the very fabric of space itself, like a cosmic flower coming to life. These nebulous gardens, where new stars are born, pulsed with vibrant energy, floating through the void like ethereal giants in a celestial garden.

Every so often, a comet streaked across the sky, a brilliant, fiery shard of light trailing a shimmering tail of cosmic dust like a messenger from the depths of space. It was as if the universe itself had sent a fleeting note of wonder, a spark that caught the eyes of those who dared to look up and dream.

The air beneath the heavens seemed alive with the hum of the cosmos, an unspoken song resonating through the stars. It was the music of the spheres, ancient and harmonious, vibrating through the fabric of time and space and reaching the earth like the echo of an unsung lullaby. It was the sound of infinity, soft yet profound, as if the universe were out there, touching each soul with its vastness and stretching mystery.

The night was deep, endless. It whispered of things beyond comprehension, galaxies swirling and colliding in distant reaches, planets unseen, and stars that flickered out in the distant past, their light now reaching our eyes. Time itself felt distant, caught in the pull of the gravitational tides, bending and warping under the infinite weight of the universe.

And yet, amid all the unfathomable vastness, there was a quiet peace. The earth below, with its fields, forests, and oceans, seemed to rest under the eternal watch of the cosmos. The night held it all, small and large, fleeting and eternal. There was a calm, an understanding, as if the stars were guardians watching over the world below, gently holding it in the folds of their light.

The night was not simply dark. It was a living, breathing universe, vast, mysterious, and full of promise. It was a dream stretched across infinity, where the past, present, and future coiled together in a single, endless spiral wrapped in the quiet majesty of the cosmos.

CHAPTER 6

The day arrived quietly, slipping in unnoticed as Estelle's alarm clock remained silent. It wasn't the first light of dawn or the fresh scent of morning that greeted her, but the piercing ring of her phone breaking the stillness. She blinked, groggy from sleep, her mind cloudy with unfinished dreams. Fumbling for the phone beside her bed, she felt its unfamiliar vibration trembling through her fingertips.

Without checking the number, she swiped to answer. "Hello?"

"Estelle?" A familiar voice came through, one she hadn't expected to hear so early, especially given the circumstances.

"Yani?" Estelle rubbed her eyes, half-dazed. The voice on the other end was softer than usual, as if it carried the warmth of something hidden. But Estelle, groggy as she was, wasn't about to miss the opportunity to check on her Yani. "Are you calling from the hospital or..." she trailed off, unsure why this number felt so foreign.

Yani's voice, tinged with an odd calmness, responded, "No, no. This is Ari's number." Estelle's brow furrowed. "Ari's number?" The surprise was almost palpable in her voice as she sat up, the sheets tangling around her. "Which Ari do you mean, the doctor?"

A brief, almost playful hesitation was on the other end of the line. "Ari, the doctor," Yani clarified, a small laugh escaping her as if she couldn't quite contain her excitement.

Estelle blinked, her mind scrambling to catch up. She hadn't expected this news, least of all at this hour. A slight chuckle left her lips. "Ah, I see. So it's that Ari," she teased, the tension from earlier beginning to melt away in the warmth of Yani's admission. "Well, well, Yani. Are you…sleeping with Ari?" she asked, a sly grin forming even though she was still half-asleep.

There was a slight pause and more uncertainty in Yani's voice. She hesitated for a moment and then softly confirmed, "Yes…I am."

The two of them erupted in laughter, the sound light and genuine, a refreshing contrast to the weight of the world outside their conversations. For a moment, it felt surreal to laugh, given everything happening outside. Estelle laughed just a little, shoulders shook with laughter, her composure wavered with the laughter she hadn't expected to share this morning.

After a few moments, Estelle calmed herself, a grin still playing on her lips as she spoke with a softer, more serious tone. "Yani, just remember to keep things low-key. The whole hospitalization story...don't let it slip too easily. It's part of the plan, and we don't want to draw any unnecessary attention to it, especially with the trial starting tomorrow. Understand?"

There was a pause before Yani's voice filtered back, a touch of reassurance in her words. "I understand, Estelle. Don't worry. I won't do anything that would jeopardize the plan."

"Good," Estelle replied, a breath of relief escaping her. "Now, about today, how are you holding up? The trial...you ready for it?"

Yani's tone shifted ever so slightly, uncertainty creeping in. "I'm...nervous. I don't know if everything will go as planned."

Estelle's voice was steady, and the confidence she needed to instill in her client rang clear. "It will go well, Yani. Just stay calm and trust in the strategy. We've planned everything meticulously, and I'm not letting them catch us off guard. The best thing you can do right now is stay composed. The trial isn't just about evidence. It's about how we present it. And you've got the strength to carry it through."

There was a long pause, and then Yani's slightly steadier voice broke the silence. "Thank you, Estelle. I'm trusting you. And...I'll keep calm."

Estelle smiled even though Yani couldn't see it, and the reassurance in her words was evident. "I know you will. And remember, the most important thing right now is to stay discreet. The more we can control the narrative, the better our chances. Just trust the plan."

Yani's tone brightened again, though there was still a trace of vulnerability. "I'll stay calm. I promise."

"Good." Estelle paused, taking a deep breath. "Now get some rest. Focus on today. And don't worry. We've got this."

Estelle ended the call and stared at the ceiling momentarily, the weight of the day finally settling onto her shoulders. The trial was hours away, and she was about to dive headfirst into the battle of a lifetime. But for a moment, she allowed herself a quiet smile at the memory of the laughter shared with Yani, a rare moment of joy before the storm. Early morning light filtered softly through the blinds, casting gentle beams across the polished wood floors of Estelle's apartment. The city outside was still quiet, with only the faint hum of distant traffic and the occasional chirp of birds breaking the serenity of the dawn. Inside, the atmosphere was calm, almost meditative.

Estelle was already awake, her mind sharp, though she hadn't yet left the comfort of her bed. Her eyes fluttered open slowly, taking in the familiar surroundings of her minimalist bedroom, sleek furniture, soft neutral tones, and the faint scent of lavender from a candle she had blown out the night before. The smooth gray duvet cocooned her as she sat up, stretching with deliberate care, her body already anticipating the day's energy ahead. It wasn't quite time to rush, but the quiet urgency of the trial loomed in the back of her mind.

She reached for the bedside table, her fingers finding the thermos of hot water she always kept by her bed. The hot liquid slid down her throat as she stared out the window momentarily, watching the first signs of life in the city, the steady rhythm of the world waking up, preparing for the bustle ahead, a moment of stillness before the storm of the courtroom.

Estelle moved toward the bathroom, her routine precise and efficient. She didn't waste time on indulgences, but something was comforting in the ritual. The water from the shower came down in a steady stream, the warm droplets cascading over her skin, washing away the remnants of sleep. She didn't linger, but the moment's solitude, the feeling of being alone in her thoughts, was grounding.

Afterward, she stood in front of the mirror, the hum of the apartment was almost louder in the silence, drying her hair with measured, confident strokes. Her reflection stared back at her, eyes that had seen countless courtroom faces and held myriad emotions, but today, they were focused and calculating. She pulled her hair back into a neat ponytail, securing it with a swift, practiced motion.

In the kitchen, the day's first task awaited: coffee. Estelle never skipped this part of her morning. She moved fluidly, her movements sharp as she ground the beans by hand, fresh, aromatic, the dark scent filling the air as the steam rose from the machine. She enjoyed the ritual: the quiet patience of waiting for the coffee to brew and anticipating that first sip. At this moment, everything felt just a bit more manageable.

While the coffee brewed, Estelle stood by the counter, going over her notes for the trial. She had already reviewed them several times the night before, but now, as the clock ticked toward the inevitable, she focused on the finer details. She flipped through the pages methodically, the words already ingrained in her mind but still needing to be committed to muscle memory. Every fact, piece of evidence, and possible angle the opposition could take was laid out before her. She had to be ready for everything.

The kettle clicked off, signaling that the coffee was ready. Estelle poured herself a cup, the deep brown liquid swirling in the mug as the steam curled upward. She added a dash of milk, her favorite way to drink coffee, strong but with enough cream to take the edge off. She took the first sip slowly, savoring the warmth that spread through her body, a small, almost intimate pleasure before the chaos of the day began.

She moved to her living room, setting the cup on the coffee table beside her tablet. The apartment, minimalist but warm, offered her peace before the battle. She leaned back into the couch's soft cushions, her mind already shifting into strategy mode. She reviewed the case in her head again, the weaknesses of the opposition, the key witnesses, and the angles they would try to exploit. Each detail needed to be perfect.

The clock on the wall ticked steadily, reminding her that time was slipping away. She checked her watch: 7:45 a.m. There was still time to get ready, but the pressure was building. Estelle took another sip of her coffee, standing up with purpose. The clothes she had chosen for today, a sharp black suit tailored to perfection, awaited her in the bedroom. Every detail had been selected with care. She needed to be poised, powerful, and unshakable. Everything she wore, everything she did would reflect that strength.

As she slipped into the suit, adjusting the blazer with practiced ease, she looked at herself in the mirror again. The reflection that met her was composed, almost unreadable, her eyes focused, unwavering. She was ready. The trial was coming, and she had already won the first battle: the preparation.

One last look at the clock: 8:15 a.m. Time to go. Estelle grabbed her briefcase, checked her phone for any last-minute updates, and made her way to the door, the weight of the day pressing on her shoulders. But she didn't falter. She never did.

Estelle stepped out of her apartment, locking the door behind her with a click. The cool morning air hit her face as she descended the stairs, her steps purposeful but light. The trial loomed, but she had a few minutes to chat with her team, her safety net, her support. They'd been working together for months, and today, their cohesion was more critical than ever.

She slid into the driver's seat of her car, the familiar scent of leather and the low hum of the engine grounding her. The dashboard clock read 8:30 a.m., so she had plenty of time to make a few calls and reassure herself that everyone was in top form.

Her first call went to David, her uncle, colleague, and the team's backbone. His deep voice came through immediately. "Morning, Estelle. You awake already?" he asked, a hint of teasing in his tone.

Estelle smiled, the tension in her shoulders easing just a bit. "You know me, I'm always up before the sun. How about you? Ready for the circus?"

David chuckled, the sound warm and familiar. "I've been ready since last night. I'm just making sure I don't trip over my notes. The court's not ready for us."

"Good," Estelle replied, a playful edge to her voice. "Remember, no impressions of the judge this time. No 'accidentally' throwing a folder on the floor."

"Oh, come on. That was one time! And it wasn't an accident," David teased back, but his tone showed a glint of pride. "Anyway, everything's set on my end. How about you? You feel the pressure yet?"

She couldn't help but laugh. "A little, but it's nothing I can't handle. You know I live for this." "Then let's give them hell. I'll see you at the courthouse in thirty."

"Deal," Estelle said before hanging up. She felt a rush of warmth from the exchange, David always knew how to make her feel like they could take on the world together.

Next, she dialed Fael, one of the team's most reliable and often quietest members. He picked up after the first ring.

"Estelle?" His voice was soft and measured.

"Morning, Fael! How's everything looking on your end?"

"Everything's prepared. Documents are in order, no surprises. I double-checked everything."

"Good. I like surprises, just not in court. You're sure everything is tight?"

"Nothing's slipping through the cracks. You're good to go."

She grinned, leaning back in her seat as the car started rolling. "Thanks, Fael. You're the best. Don't let anyone rattle you today, all right?"

"Never," he replied with a small laugh. "See you soon."

"See you there."

The next call went to Christina. The two had worked together for years, and Estelle was always glad to hear her friend's voice.

"Christina, you up?"

"Of course, I'm up. Do you think I will let you face this trial without me?" Christina's voice was as sharp as ever but had an underlying warmth.

"I wouldn't dream of it," Estelle said, smiling. "How's everything looking? Are you all set with the strategy?"

"Everything's locked in," Christina said confidently. "I've gone over the defense arguments one more time. There are no mistakes today. And hey, just a heads-up, I heard the opposition's team is still arguing over some details. Looks like we've already thrown them off-balance."

"Good. Keep them guessing." Estelle couldn't help but feel the spark of victory. "Oh, and remember, try not to be so intimidating. The jury will fear you before the witnesses even take the stand."

Christina laughed, a low sound that made Estelle's heart lift. "If only they knew how intimidating I am when I'm wearing heels."

"See you at ten, partner. Let's make some magic happen."

Estelle ended the call, feeling the last lingering doubts about the day melt away.

There was one last call. Her final check-in was with Carlos, a rising star in the firm who had been handling some of the background work. His quiet confidence made Estelle trust him implicitly.

"Carlos, are you awake? Or am I catching you mid-snooze?"

There was a brief pause before Carlos's voice came through. "I don't need much sleep, Estelle. I'm good to go. Everything's been double-checked, the evidence, the witness prep. We've got this."

"I like hearing that. You feeling all right?" Estelle's tone softened, genuine concern slipping through.

"I'm great. Just…trying to stay calm, you know?"

"Yeah, I get that. But listen, today is our day. We've got the upper hand, and we're ready for anything. Just don't let them see you sweat. They'll try to get under your skin, but we won't let them."

Carlos chuckled. "Don't worry, I've been practicing my poker face."

"Good. You've got this. I'll see you in the courtroom."

Estelle hung up, the weight of the trial still there but lighter now. She had her team, strong, prepared, and ready for anything.

Estelle placed her phone down and took a deep breath. The courthouse was only a few minutes away now, and the time for preparation was over. It was time to put everything she had planned into motion.

Estelle felt the familiar pulse of excitement in her veins, the thrill of a challenge, the joy of the game. The trial was about to begin, and she was ready to face it head-on.

Estelle parked her car in the underground lot, the engine's purring slowly fading as she turned off the ignition. The air outside was heavy with the buzz of anticipation, the kind of charged energy that filled the streets when something monumental was about to happen.

As she exited her car, she felt the day's weight descend into her bones. With a practiced hand, she adjusted her blazer and gazed at the tall courthouse. The stone facade loomed overhead, silently observing the scene unfolding inside. Outside, throngs had already formed, journalists with cameras ready, activists brandishing colorful signs, and inquisitive passersby anxious to see the spectacle. The trial had become a standalone public event.

Estelle's heels clicked against the pavement as she walked toward the entrance, her steps purposeful, but there was no mistaking the attention she drew. Whispers rippled through the crowd. "That's Estelle, she's the one leading the defense!" A reporter shouted her name, but Estelle didn't flinch, her face a perfect mask of calm professionalism.

A cheer went up as she passed, a small rally of supporters and admirers cheering her on. It wasn't uncommon for Estelle to be seen as a star in the legal world, but today, the attention felt different. Today, her skills, reputation, and everything she had built were on the line. She gave the crowd a slight acknowledging nod but focused straight ahead.

Entering the courthouse, Estelle was immediately struck by the contrast between the bustling crowds outside and the cold, imposing silence within. The long corridors were filled with people moving in all directions, attorneys rushing to their cases, officers stationed at regular intervals, and groups of eager spectators making their way to the public seating areas.

As Estelle moved deeper into the courthouse, her presence didn't go unnoticed. Several heads turned in her direction. Then, as she reached the grand doors of the courtroom, something peculiar happened. She was intercepted by Prosecutor Colonne and her assistant, both standing with exaggerated smiles, their expressions disturbingly pleasant.

"Estelle!" Colonne called out, her voice carrying a false cheer that immediately set Estelle on edge. "A pleasure to see you this fine morning."

Estelle paused, her eyebrow quirked in suspicion as she glanced at Colonne, a woman known for her sharp, often underhanded tactics. The fact that she was being so unusually amiable felt wrong.

"Colonne," Estelle said, her tone polite but cautious. "I didn't expect such a warm welcome. Should I be concerned?"

"Oh, not at all," Colonne responded with a smile that didn't quite reach her eyes. Her assistant beside her mirrored her expression, a slight, tight-lipped grin that sent a chill down Estelle's spine. "Just wanted to wish you good luck today. We both know how things go when it's time to make your case."

Estelle's instincts were heightened, and she felt uneasy. Why were they acting so friendly? She couldn't put her finger on it, but something felt off. Before she could respond, her attention was drawn to the corridor ahead.

A group of magistrates, notorious for their questionable moral compass, were standing by the door leading to the office of the senior judge. They laughed too loudly, speaking in low tones with gestures almost too jovial for the occasion. Estelle's eyes narrowed as she observed them. What were they doing here? These were the kind of people who'd bend the law to suit their own needs, and they had no business being near the senior judge's chambers. This was not a coincidence.

Her mind raced as she processed the scene before her. Was there something she hadn't accounted for? Were these magistrates part of some hidden agenda?

Before she could investigate further, her colleagues arrived in the hallway, walking with quick, purposeful strides. David, Christina, Fael, and Carlos appeared well-prepared, focused, and ready for what lay ahead. The familiar faces brought her a sense of relief even though the situation felt increasingly tense.

"Estelle," David said, catching sight of her. He smiled, but there was a knowing look in his eyes, a silent exchange of understanding that the weight of the trial was heavy on them all. "You good?"

Estelle glanced back toward the group of magistrates, then to Colonne and her assistant, who were still standing with unsettling smiles. She gestured subtly for her team to gather around her, and they did so quickly, creating a small circle.

"We have a problem," Estelle whispered, her voice low enough that only they could hear. "Those magistrates…they're up to something. I've never seen them work behind the scenes, and I don't trust them. They're too close to the senior judge, and I don't know what they're planning."

Christina's eyes hardened as she took in the sight of the magistrate group.

The door to the courtroom creaked slightly as Estelle and her team entered, stepping onto the cool marble floor with quiet, deliberate steps. The air inside was thick with anticipation, every seat in the gallery was filled, every corner of the room alive with whispers. Journalists, photographers, and spectators crowded around the elevated seats in the back, their attention fixed on the defense table where Estelle now stood. The usual tension of a high-profile trial was amplified today, as if the walls held their breath.

Estelle walked confidently to her place, her heels clicking against the floor with purpose. The prosecution's table, directly opposite, was already filled with Colonne, her assistant, and a few of her most trusted staff members. Their presence was almost too calm, too collected, as if they were waiting for something to unfold that Estelle didn't yet understand.

The judge's seat loomed at the front of the courtroom, a symbol of authority that was hard to ignore. Estelle glanced at the senior judge's bench as she approached her seat. The senior judge was already present, her black robes contrasting with the crisp white paperwork scattered before her. The look on the judge's face was unreadable. Still, something was unsettling about how she was eyeing the room, her eyes darting between Colonne, the assistant, and the group of magistrates still lingering outside the door.

Estelle's heart quickened. It didn't take a seasoned lawyer to know that something was off. The group of morally dubious magistrates she had seen earlier in the corridor were sitting together, their eyes fixed on her with an intensity that sent a shiver down her spine.

They deliberately avoided eye contact with the judge, almost as if waiting for a signal. Estelle's instincts screamed at her to be wary. If they were involved in the trial's outcome, the scales of justice might already be tipped in a direction she couldn't predict.

"Is everything all right?" Christina whispered, leaning over to Estelle as she sat beside her.

Estelle glanced at the magistrates again but quickly turned her focus back to the judge. "I'm not sure yet. Just stay sharp."

The court clerk called the proceedings to order, his voice cutting through the low murmur of the room. "All rise. The honorable court is now in session."

The room fell into immediate silence, the atmosphere growing heavier as the judge took her seat. Estelle's team straightened, instinctively aligning themselves for what was to come. She could hear her heart beating in her chest, but she kept her exterior calm, knowing that any sign of weakness could be exploited.

The judge, Senior Judge Djonga, raised her gavel and gave it a single firm tap, signaling the start of the trial. "We are here today to hear the defense's arguments regarding Yani versus the state. Prosecutor Colonne, please proceed."

Colonne rose smoothly to her feet, her posture immaculate. Her expression was composed, too composed. There was an air of confidence around her, but it felt too rehearsed, as though she knew something that Estelle didn't.

The courtroom was charged with a strange, simmering energy, and the air was thick with anticipation. Estelle sat poised, tapping the table's edge. Her eyes locked onto the prosecutor, Colonne. She was standing at the podium now, her posture unnaturally straight, like an actor in a play, ready to deliver her next line. But what subtly came next felt like the beginning of a dark, twisted comedy.

"Your Honor," Colonne began, her voice honeyed and smooth, dripping with false concern, "before we proceed with the facts at hand, I would like to address a crucial element that might shed light on the defendant's, shall we say, character."

Estelle's brow furrowed. Character? She leaned forward slightly, her eyes narrowing as Colonne continued, her tone rising theatrically.

"It seems, Your Honor, that the defendant, Ms. Yani, has exhibited behaviors that suggest a profound disconnection from her colleagues. This goes beyond a simple preference for privacy," Colonne said, pacing with a calculated air of gravitas. "It is, in fact, a clear and troubling pattern of social withdrawal."

The words struck the room like a slap, leaving the spectators, the press, and even the judge stunned. Estelle's heart skipped a beat. What was she talking about?

Colonne's eyes flicked toward the lawyers at the defense table, her expression feigning pity. "Ms. Yani is not here and refuses to participate in basic social activities at work. She avoids birthday parties. She turns down invitations to casual dinners. She does not attend office gatherings, not even for the court trial. Now, tell me, Your Honor, what does such behavior suggest? What could a person like this be hiding?"

There was a moment of eerie silence. The room seemed to shrink, the walls pressing in. This...this was the case?

Estelle glanced at her colleagues. David's face was a mixture of confusion and disbelief, his mouth slightly agape. Christina's brow was furrowed in concern, and even Fael's ever-calm demeanor cracked for just a moment, his eyes wide as if he couldn't quite process what he was hearing.

The prosecutor continued, her voice a strange mixture of mock sympathy and thinly veiled accusation. "Is she too good for the people she works with, Your Honor? Is her refusal to engage with others a sign of guilt? Is this the behavior of a leader? Or is it the behavior of someone who has something to hide? Something far darker?"

Estelle's jaw clenched so tightly she felt her teeth hurt. This was absurd. What was this about? Was Colonne making a case based on office parties in front of the judge and the public? Didn't Yani attend a few social gatherings?

A murmur rippled through the courtroom, and the public was as baffled as Estelle's team. Some shook their heads, unsure of what they had just heard. Others whispered among themselves, trying to make sense of Colonne's bizarre accusations.

But Estelle's patience was wearing thin. She couldn't let this continue.

"Your Honor." She stood up, and her voice **was** cold and sharp. "This is not only irrelevant, it's utterly ridiculous. We are here to address serious accusations, not whether my client attended a party!"

She turned toward the judge, her voice rising in frustration. "This is a legal proceeding, not a high school popularity contest! These allegations have nothing to do with the charges against Ms. Yani. How can we take this seriously?"

Unable to contain his disbelief, David leaned forward and added, "Your Honor, I must ask, are we seriously entertaining the idea that whether Ms. Yani attends a colleague's birthday party has anything to do with the case? This is an utter waste of this court's time!"

The courtroom, still heavy with confusion, seemed to hold its breath. All eyes were now on the judge, who had remained silent until now.

But then, to Estelle's shock, Judge Djonga didn't even look at her. The judge's gaze remained fixed on Colonne, who was now watching Estelle with an unreadable smile, one that was almost too broad, too satisfied.

The judge's lips parted slowly, and in a voice that was as flat and unfeeling as the steel gavel beside her, she spoke, "Ms. Colonne, I find your argument compelling. Please, continue."

Estelle's heart pounded in her chest. *Compelling?* She couldn't believe her ears. Was the judge agreeing with this madness?

David let out a frustrated breath, his eyes flashing with anger. "Your Honor, please! This is a complete mockery of the law. These complaints are not evidence. They're petty personal grievances, gossip at best!"

The judge didn't respond to him. She barely even acknowledged his protest. Instead, she waved a hand, dismissing the objection with a single motion.

"Ms. Colonne, proceed," Judge Djonga said again, her voice as cold as the marble bench she sat behind.

Estelle's eyes widened. What was happening?

David, clearly fuming, leaned toward Estelle and whispered sharply, "This is getting ridiculous. We need to shut this down now, or it will spiral completely out of control," his voice laced with frustration and disbelief.

Estelle didn't respond immediately, her mind racing as Colonne continued to speak, almost smugly now, with the court's full attention. She could feel the weight of the audience's stares, the confusion and discomfort in the air growing palpable.

"Thank you, Your Honor," Colonne said, adjusting her glasses and turning toward the jury, then addressing them as though delivering the punchline of a twisted joke. "Now, as we have established, Ms. Yani's social isolation is not just a passing behavior. It's an indicator of deeper issues. This is a woman who has no connection with her peers, who refuses to integrate into society, and who hides behind the shield of introversion." She paused dramatically. "One might even say this is the hallmark of someone concealing their true nature, someone with something to hide."

Estelle's blood ran cold. She gripped the edge of her table so tightly that her knuckles turned white. What was she trying to do? Paint Yani as a cold, distant person who didn't fit into societal norms and somehow twist this into something damning?

David's hand shot up in the air, his voice filled with rage that couldn't be contained. "Objection! Objection, Your Honor! This is not only irrelevant, it's borderline nonsensical. Social preferences are not criminal behavior!" He was on his feet now, his chair crashing back into the floor. "We are here for facts, not speculative nonsense about a person's private life!"

The judge's face didn't flicker. She waved her hand in the air, a dismissive gesture that seemed to come far too quickly. "Mr. David, your objection is noted, but we will continue," Judge Djonga intoned, her voice flat and devoid of empathy. She leaned forward just slightly, her eyes cold and disinterested. "Ms. Colonne, proceed with your questioning."

David's jaw tightened. The rest of the defense team exchanged worried glances. Christina, always the composed one, finally spoke in a low voice. "This is insane. The judge's refusal to listen, it's like they're already playing their hand."

Estelle turned sharply, her voice barely above a whisper but sharp with urgency. "Hold on. Don't give up just yet." Her mind was racing, desperate to find some way to shift the tide. There had to be a way to turn this around.

Meanwhile, Colonne, now emboldened by the judge's tacit approval, was practically relishing the moment. She smiled to herself before continuing with the same sinister tone. "Your Honor, I also wish to point out that Ms. Yani's detachment is not limited to her professional life. This same behavior is evident in her relationships. I have learned, through sources I cannot name, that she has no significant friendships, no ties to any social group. She isolates herself in her personal time as well."

The room seemed to hold its breath. The murmurs started again, people exchanged puzzled glances, trying to make sense of this strange turn of events. Sources she couldn't name? Estelle's mind reeled. How was any of this admissible?

Estelle rose sharply from her seat, her chair scraping loudly against the floor. She couldn't take it any longer. "Your Honor, with all due respect, I must ask, where are the facts? Where is the evidence? We're hearing about parties and social events that have no bearing whatsoever on the charges against my client! This is not a circus! This is a courtroom!"

Judge Djonga's eyes finally shifted to her, but her expression was as indifferent as ever. "Ms. Estelle, you are emotional. Your client's conduct is being evaluated, and I see no reason to stop this line of questioning." She turned her gaze back to Colonne, her eyes narrowing slightly. "Proceed."

Estelle stood frozen, her blood boiling. She could feel the court swirling around her, sinking deeper into the absurdity. The judge wasn't even pretending to be impartial anymore.

But David wasn't done. He stepped forward again, his voice cutting through the tension. "Objection! This is not a character trial! The prosecutor is making unfounded claims with no evidence to support them! We are here for facts, not baseless accusations based on someone's social calendar!"

There was a long silence. The judge's cold gaze remained fixed on David. Then, to everyone's surprise, Judge Djonga slowly leaned back in her chair, her fingers steepled in front of her face as she observed the proceedings with an almost unnervingly calm demeanor.

"You are welcome to make your objections, Mr. David," she said, her voice softer now but still chilling in its aloofness. "But the nature of the defendant's behavior is directly relevant to her mental state, which is a matter of great importance."

Estelle's heart pounded in her chest. This was a nightmare. There was no logic to it, no semblance of justice.

The courtroom had become something unrecognizable. The once-serene atmosphere was now charged with a chaotic energy that bordered on madness. The prosecution had devolved into a bizarre charade, and Judge Djonga seemed content to let the absurdity unfold.

Seizing the moment, Colonne stood up again with an air of gravitas, her voice cutting through the tension. "Your Honor," she said, her eyes glinting with the thrill of her latest move, "I would like to call a witness to the stand, a man who has information that could shed light on the nature of the defendant's behavior."

Estelle's eyes narrowed. A witness? Where had Colonne found him? It seemed that she was reaching for anything at this point.

A few moments later, an older man shuffled forward, his slow, deliberate steps echoing in the courtroom's silence. His hunched back and frail frame indicated that he was well past his prime, but his eyes were wide and alert, though they revealed a hint of confusion.

He was sworn in with all the pomp and formality of a regular witness, but there was an undeniable air of absurdity about the whole thing. The man adjusted his glasses, peered at the room as though he had no idea where he was, and then looked at Colonne, who was positively beaming.

"Do you know the defendant, Ms. Yani?" Colonne asked, her voice smooth and rehearsed, as though delivering a line in a play.

The older man scratched his head for a moment, then nodded slowly. "Yes, yes, I know her," he said, his voice shaky, as though he wasn't entirely sure of himself. "She…she works with my niece, I believe." He squinted, trying to recall something, anything. "Yes, yes, that's right. She's the one who…who… what was it? Oh, yes! She came to the office a few times."

Colonne smiled smugly. "And did you ever speak to her?"

The older man blinked, his brow furrowing as though he was trying to grasp the question. "Oh, I…I think she once gave me a brochure about office supplies. Or was it a calendar?" He seemed utterly lost. "Yes, I'm sure that was her, but I don't remember much after that. She seemed very… busy."

The courtroom was so still you could hear the man's rambling thoughts hanging in the air. Colonne pressed on, her tone unwavering. "So you do know Ms. Yani?" The older man nodded with a slow, deliberate motion. "Yes, yes, I do. But…" He scratched his head again. "Wait. You're the one who told me to come here and say I knew her."

The words hung in the air like an impossible riddle. The courtroom was momentarily silent, waiting for someone to scream that this couldn't happen.

Then someone, Estelle wasn't sure who, chuckled nervously. Was this a joke?

The frail old man continued, "I've never really talked to her much, you know? But you told me to say I knew her. I think it was for this trial. You gave me instructions, didn't you?"

A ripple of laughter spread through the courtroom. Some reporters exchanged incredulous glances while others barely stifled their amusement. The absurdity of the situation had become too much for many to ignore.

But to Estelle's utter horror, Judge Djonga remained unfazed. Instead of intervening, she leaned forward, her eyes gleaming with an odd satisfaction. "Yes, yes," she said with an eerie calm. "This witness is indeed obvious in his answers. He's answered all questions quite brightly, I must say."

The judge's tone was so unnervingly approving that Estelle felt a chill crawl up her spine. How could anyone be taking this seriously? Was this some sick joke?

David, his face flushed with disbelief, leaned toward Estelle again. "What the hell is going on?

This is like a circus. What is Colonne even trying to do here?"

Before Estelle could respond, Colonne was back on her feet, nodding enthusiastically at the judge. "Thank you, Your Honor. This testimony is vital to understanding the defendant's complex character."

Estelle's fists clenched. This wasn't a trial. This was a mockery.

The older man was escorted off the stand, but Colonne, utterly unshaken, immediately called for another witness. "Your Honor, I request that we now hear from the next individual, a woman who may hold crucial insights into Ms. Yani's true nature."

A woman in her mid-thirties, wearing a bright floral dress, appeared in the doorway. She entered with a broad smile, her eyes darting around nervously. She looked entirely out of place, like she had mistakenly wandered into the wrong room.

"Who are you?" Colonne asked, her tone as smooth as ever but with an underlying hint of accusation. "What do you know about the defendant, Ms. Yani?"

The woman blinked at her, her smile faltering. "Uh, I'm…I'm sorry, but…I don't know why I'm here. I…I was just told to come and…and speak." She glanced around the room, clearly confused. "I don't even know who Ms. Yani is."

The boy emerged from the shadows of the courtroom, slipping between the rows of spectators and lawyers like a ghost. His movements were subtle, almost imperceptible, but his gait showed an unmistakable sense of urgency. His wide eyes, darting from side to side, betrayed his unease in the buzzing atmosphere of the trial. He looked out of place, too young, too disoriented, but his stride had a quiet determination, as if he had a task to do and nothing else mattered.

She saw the boy approaching, a file clutched tightly in his hands.

The boy didn't look directly at her as he approached, but she could feel the intensity of his gaze. His steps were careful, his shoes barely making a sound on the polished floor. He leaned in slightly as he reached her table, just enough for Estelle to catch his movement. His hand extended the file in his palm.

Estelle's fingers gripped the file when the young teenager handed it to her. The boy, no older than fifteen, had approached her quietly as if delivering a secret too essential to be spoken aloud. He didn't make eye contact, just silently pointed toward the exit where a large crowd of spectators and journalists clustered.

"A policeman," he said, the faintest hint of urgency in his voice.

Estelle looked toward the door, but she couldn't see anyone. The room was alive with noise: the murmur of a hundred whispered conversations, the clattering keyboards, and the press scribbling furiously. The young boy turned to leave quickly as if to disappear into the crowd.

She unfolded the five pages carefully. Her eyes skimmed over the first few lines, and something in her gut twisted. Her breath caught in her throat.

She immediately passed the file to David, sitting next to her, observing the absurdity of the trial with growing frustration. He took the file with a raised eyebrow, a silent question in his eyes. Estelle nodded subtly, encouraging him to read. His expression shifted from curiosity to concentration as he flipped through the pages.

Two minutes passed, minutes that felt like hours, and then David stood up suddenly, his chair scraping across the floor. His face was hard, a mask of silent resolve, and without a word, he walked toward the primary judge.

The room seemed to freeze momentarily as everyone turned to watch David approach. Estelle's heart hammered in her chest. What was going on? The trial was already a circus, but something unexpected was now happening.

David spoke briefly to the judge. Estelle couldn't hear their words, but from how the judge's eyes narrowed in surprise, she could tell this wasn't a routine conversation. After a tense few moments, the judge nodded stiffly, her face impassive, and gestured for David to follow her.

Estelle watched, almost unable to believe what she was witnessing, as David stepped into a corridor with the primary judge. But that wasn't the end. The door to the office they'd entered was already closing behind them when Estelle's gaze was drawn to a figure on the other side of the room, a policeman.

This tall, broad-shouldered policeman had just received a signal and walked briskly toward the prosecutor's table. His movements were deliberate, and his face was stern. Colonne stood, a look of barely concealed surprise crossing her face as the policeman addressed her with a brief whisper. Colonne's lips tightened, and her expression faltered momentarily before she composed herself and slowly nodded at the signal from the judge's office.

Without a word, Colonne stood and followed the policeman toward the same office David and the judge had entered. It was too much. Estelle's mind raced. What was happening?

The room's murmurs grew louder as the courtroom seemed to shift from confusion to suspicion. The group of magistrates who had been laughing earlier, those same magistrates who had been part of the surreal charade in the courtroom, stood up suddenly. Their laughter died, replaced by a collective eagerness. They too followed Colonne and the policeman into the office.

Estelle couldn't believe her eyes. This was no longer a trial but a farce on the verge of collapse. She could hear some spectators in the room shouting angrily, their voices trembling with frustration.

"Stop your fraud!" one man yelled. "This is a mockery!" another voice added, followed by a chorus of agreement from several others in the room. The tension was palpable, and Estelle could feel it in her bones.

The courtroom felt on the verge of exploding. There was no way to pretend that this was even close to a fair trial. Colonne and her cohorts had already lost the room, yet Colonne still seemed to believe they could control the narrative.

Estelle leaned toward Christina, who had been watching in stunned silence. The others gathered around her, exchanging confused glances.

"What do you think this means?" Christina asked, her voice low but cautiously optimistic.

Estelle's heart still raced, but she couldn't ignore the strange sense of hope beginning to build within her. Something was shifting. David knew what he was doing. They had new information, accurate information that could make a difference. Before Estelle could respond, David came back into the room. His face was tense, but a glint in his eyes spoke of something significant he hadn't yet shared.

He walked straight to the table, and the courtroom seemed to hold its breath as he began to speak, his voice steady. "The trial has been postponed. The judge has called for a recess until 2:00 p.m."

Estelle felt relief wash over her, tempered by the uncertainty of what had just happened. "Postponed?" she asked, her voice barely above a whisper.

David nodded, his expression unreadable. "Yes. The judge has ordered a break."

CHAPTER 7

David's voice broke the silence that had fallen over the group of lawyers. His usual calm demeanor was replaced with a rare tension as he gathered the team around him, his eyes scanning each face before he spoke.

"We need to discuss something important," he said, his words breaking through the uneasy buzz in the room. Estelle looked up from the documents she had been poring over, her mind still reeling from the absurdity of the trial and the bizarre turn of events. Despite the chaos, the courtroom had fallen eerily silent as everyone awaited David's next words.

David opened his briefcase, pulling out five pages, the same ones the young boy had delivered to Estelle moments ago. His fingers hovered over the papers for a moment before he set them down in front of the group, one by one. The atmosphere in the room shifted, becoming more serious, more intense.

"These documents..." he began, pausing momentarily as if to gather his thoughts, "they are a letter from the president to Judge Djonga, requesting that the trial be stopped."

The team exchanged confused and cautious glances. Estelle leaned forward, trying to piece it together. The president? Why would the president of the Republic get involved in a case like this?

Carlos, always quick to ask the questions on everyone's mind, raised his hand almost impatiently. "Why would the president want this trial stopped? What does this have to do with us or Yani?"

David's expression hardened. "Because a man has sent the president a vast, top-secret file containing explosive information about the state's dark dealings. In that file, there is a message and a warning. The man has threatened to release these documents to international diplomatic representatives, journalists, activists, everyone. He says that the truth will be exposed to the world if Yani does not receive a fair trial."

Estelle felt the weight of his words sink into her. The truth? What was in those files? And who had sent them?

David continued, his voice growing more intense. "The message is clear: if Yani doesn't get a just trial, this person will send the files to everyone, every country, every organization, every journalist. And the state's secrets, the real truth, will be out in the open."

The realization hit like a thunderclap. The stakes had just risen exponentially. This wasn't just about one woman's case. This was about everything, exposing corruption and unmasking the state's darkest secrets. The trial, which had already felt like a farce, had suddenly become the epicenter of something much more significant that could rock the entire political landscape.

The room fell silent again as each lawyer processed this new information. The implications were staggering. The president was involved. The police were involved. And now, the very course of the trial was at risk of being influenced by forces much more significant than anyone had anticipated.

"Are we supposed to believe this?" Carlos asked, his voice a mixture of disbelief and concern. "How do we even know if this is real?"

David nodded grimly, his gaze shifting to the letter from the president. "I spoke to someone who confirmed the existence of these files. The man who sent them to the president is legitimate. His warning is real. This isn't just a bluff."

There was a long pause as the weight of the situation settled over them.

Estelle felt a sickening sense of foreboding. The state was being threatened, its secrets exposed, and they were all caught in the middle.

A sharp and anxious voice from the back of the room interrupted the moment. "So what does this mean for us? Are we supposed to make a deal? A compromise?"

David's eyes narrowed. "I've been thinking about that and don't like where this is headed. They want a compromise, a deal to stop the chaos. The government, the judges, and the prosecutor are all involved in this, and now they're scrambling to make things go away quietly."

He paused for effect, letting the words sink in. "But we can't just accept this, not for Yani or justice. This trial has already been manipulated too much. The judge, the prosecutor, they've played a game with us. We cannot allow them to cover this up with some half-baked compromise."

The group murmured in angry agreement, each profoundly aware of the injustices they'd witnessed.

Christina, always the pragmatic one, spoke up, her voice low but firm. "David's right. This isn't just about Yani anymore. It's about everyone who's ever been wronged by this system. We've been fighting for a fair trial, and now it's become a fight for something bigger: the truth. We cannot let them use this as a bargaining chip."

Fael, usually reserved, leaned forward, his voice trembling with quiet fury. "We can't just let them sweep this under the rug. No compromise. The state doesn't get to play this game and then walk away without consequence."

As Estelle's colleagues stood united in their decision, the door of the courtroom opened, and a quiet hush swept across the room. Yani, dressed in a modest but professional outfit, walked in with

Ari. Her posture was **strong**, but her eyes betrayed the toll of the past weeks. The courtroom, once filled with noise, seemed to hold its breath as they entered.

Estelle glanced at her client, her heart heavy with Yani's burden. Ari's presence beside her was a silent but solid reminder of the support she had, someone who had fought for her when no one else had. Estelle was reminded once more of why they were here, not just for a trial, but for a revolution of justice.

The judge had just finished speaking with the prosecutor, Colonne, and the tension in the room was palpable. Judge Djonga's eyes flickered toward Yani as she sat beside Estelle. For the first time in the entire trial, Estelle saw a flash of something in the judge's gaze, perhaps fear, perhaps anticipation. But there was no time to dwell on it. David, who had been standing near the defense table, gave a subtle nod to Estelle. The trial was about to resume.

The moment the proceedings started again, Colonne stood, her high heels clicking almost mockingly as she took her place at the podium. She cleared her throat theatrically, eyes sweeping over the room as if relishing the attention. However, the room was no longer in her control.

David leaned forward slightly, his expression unreadable, but his fingers tapped lightly against the table, a silent signal. It was time.

Colonne opened her mouth to speak, but before she could begin her usual tirade, David stood and cut her off calmly but commandingly. "Your Honor, before we proceed, we would like to address some new developments, new evidence that has come to light."

The room fell silent again. All eyes were now on David. The prosecutor's face twitched, her lips pressing into a tight line. She wasn't prepared for this. Judge Djonga glanced up, her cold, calculating gaze falling on David.

"Proceed," she said, her voice distant, as though she was barely paying attention.

David didn't hesitate. "We have just received confirmation of a message sent to the president of the Republic. The president himself has been made aware of the situation and, more importantly, the top-secret files that were sent to him detailing significant misconduct within the state. These documents were sent alongside a direct warning that if Detective Yani does not receive a fair and impartial trial, these files will be released to international diplomatic representatives, journalists, and activists. This is not just an empty threat. It's a promise from someone who has the power to expose the state's darkest secrets."

A murmur of disbelief swept through the room. The audience was captivated, their heads turning to look at one another as if to confirm they had heard David correctly. Estelle couldn't help but notice the subtle shift in the judge's posture, a moment of uncertainty before she quickly regained her composure.

But Colonne, now visibly rattled, cleared her throat loudly. "This is completely irrelevant!" she snapped. "We are here to discuss the facts of the case, not some baseless accusations meant to divert attention from the matter at hand."

David's gaze never wavered. "It is directly relevant, Your Honor. This case has already been compromised at every level, from the courtroom to the highest offices in the land. The trial has become a spectacle, and we will not stand by while a person's life is trampled for political games."

Judge Djonga, still cold and distant, nodded almost imperceptibly, but the shift in the room's energy was undeniable. The court was no longer under Colonne's control.

"You're wasting time, David," Colonne snapped again, but her words held no weight. The crowd was buzzing, some whispering in excitement, others in disbelief. Was this all happening?

Then one of the journalists already seated near the aisle stood up. He was in his mid-thirties, wearing glasses and carrying a notepad. He moved toward the judge's bench, but his movements were slow and deliberate, a disruption.

"Your Honor, if I may," the journalist called out, holding his notepad for the judge to see. "I have received reliable information from multiple sources that documents related to this trial have already made their way into the hands of international organizations. It's only a matter of time before this reaches the press. The people have the right to know."

There was a collective gasp from the crowd. Colonne's eyes narrowed, and Estelle could see the panic creeping into her once-commanding posture.

The judge did not immediately respond to the journalist. She sat frozen momentarily, looking down at her notepad and then back at David. The weight of the situation settled over everyone like a blanket of tension.

"We are witnessing the unraveling of something far bigger than this trial," Judge Djonga began, before stopping herself.

The tension in the courtroom reached a fever pitch. Everyone was watching, waiting, for something to give. The very air seemed charged, thick with anticipation. Yet what happened next was nothing like anyone could have predicted.

Judge Djonga, her lips pressed tightly together, stared at the documents on her bench, her eyes flickering nervously between the papers and the growing crowd in the room. It was as if the weight of her decisions had suddenly become too much to bear. The grim, unshakable facade that had once defined her as an untouchable figure of authority seemed to crack, piece by piece, before everyone's eyes.

She stood abruptly, her chair scraping loudly against the marble floor. The room fell into a stunned silence. She didn't even look at the defense team or the prosecutor. Her hands, trembling slightly, gripped the sides of her robe, and her usually composed face paled. It was clear: she had lost control.

"Court is adjourned," Judge Djonga declared, her voice devoid of the commanding force it once held.

It was a declaration made with a weary, almost defeated tone, as if she had already accepted the inevitable. There was no explanation, no reasoning, just the cold, final words that echoed through the room.

The entire room seemed to collapse under her command. The journalists, the spectators, and the activists, all of them stood in stunned silence. The judge's once-stiff posture now appeared fragile, like a statue crumbling under pressure.

But it wasn't just the judge who had faltered. Prosecutor Colonne, who had been so unshakable just moments earlier, stood at her podium, her face flushed with anger and humiliation. Her usual self-assuredness had vanished. She looked at the judge, then the defense team, and finally back to the crowd, her eyes darting around as if she were searching for an escape route. Her lips trembled with the frustration of someone who had been outplayed, but she couldn't find the words.

Colonne straightened her back without glancing at the lawyers, her posture stiff with forced dignity. But there was nothing dignified in her hasty retreat. She grabbed the papers in front of her and, without another word, hurried to the side door, her heels clicking sharply against the floor in a desperate rhythm.

As Colonne exited, her movement was hurried, almost frantic, as though she had no more defenses left to give. Her body language screamed of defeat, of someone running, not from the truth, but from the consequences of her actions.

The judges, who had spent the entire morning chuckling and exchanging whispers in the back corners of the room, fell silent now. Their faces drained of color, and they rose as if in unspoken agreement. They too gathered their things and moved toward the door, muttering to one another as they made their swift exit, leaving behind the very people they were supposed to serve. The corruption, the games they had played, all of it was unraveling now.

The room was filled with an uncomfortable silence. The buzz of the audience died down as people began to exchange confused glances. What was happening? Why was the trial ending like this? The judge and prosecutor had run away; they hadn't explained or offered any reasoning for the sudden adjournment.

It wasn't just a failed trial. It was the collapse of an entire system, crumbling in real time before the public eye. It was a spectacle, absurd and almost surreal in its quiet finality. The very people who had orchestrated this mess were now slipping out of the room without so much as a word.

David stood, watching the judge's hasty exit, his face impassive but his eyes dark with the moment's weight. His hand rested on the table as if to steady himself.

Estelle couldn't believe what she saw. She turned to her colleagues, exchanging looks, but no one seemed to know what to do next. The trial was over, but no one knew why or if it would ever resume.

Finally, Yani broke the silence, her voice shaking with disbelief and relief. "Is it...over?"

David nodded, his voice low and thoughtful. "For today, yes. But it's not over, not by a long shot."

The lawyers gathered their things, moving to leave the courtroom. Still reeling from the sudden collapse, the spectators stood slowly and began filing out, murmuring. Their voices were filled with the same confusion, the same uncertainty.

Justice had taken a strange, almost absurd turn today. The institution supposed to uphold the law had cracked open in front of everyone, and now, this broken system was scattered across the courtroom floor.

But as David said, it wasn't over. They had no intention of letting it end here. The files, the truth, and the essence of what they were fighting for, were still out there, waiting to come to light.

Estelle could feel the day's weight pressing down on her as she walked alongside Yani and the rest of the team. The judge and prosecutor had fled, but they hadn't won, not yet. The battle was far from over. And Estelle knew this was only the beginning of something far more monumental than anyone in that room could comprehend.

And with that, they exited the courtroom together, united, determined, and ready for whatever would come next.

As the room buzzed with the chaotic energy of the crowd, Estelle and her colleagues made their way out of the courtroom, the cacophony of voices ringing in their ears. Supporters of the defense team stood in solidarity, shouting words of encouragement, while the journalists, particularly those from state-controlled media, clung to the walls. They avoided making eye contact, their faces painted with discomfort and denial.

Sharp-eyed and quick to seize an opportunity, Christina spotted one of the most familiar faces in the press corps, a lady journalist known for her close ties to the ruling elite and a prominent fixture in the government's public relations machine. The woman had always carried herself with an air of arrogance, her columns written with a certain arrogance and disregard for the truth Christina had long come to despise.

Seeing the tides of public opinion turning against the system she had been so loyal to, the lady journalist began to slink toward the exit, her eyes darting nervously around as though trying to avoid attention. She moved with the furtive steps of someone trying to escape the consequences of their complicity.

But Christina wasn't going to let her slip away unnoticed. With a purposeful stride, Christina cut through the crowd, weaving past the supporters and avoiding the cameras now swarming around the defense team. Her eyes fixed on the journalist; she reached the side exit just as the woman went to her car, a shiny black sedan parked far from the commotion of the courtroom.

"We might have a word," Christina called out, her voice calm but steady, carrying the weight of unspoken truths.

The lady journalist froze, her hand resting on the car door handle, the tension in the air palpable. The journalist turned slowly, her face pale. She recognized Christina immediately, and for a split second, her expression faltered, a brief flicker of guilt before she masked it with a thin, professional smile.

"Christina, what a surprise," she said, her voice far too forced, as if trying to brush aside the inevitable confrontation. "I was just leaving. The day's events were…entirely unexpected, weren't they?"

Christina stepped closer, her posture unwavering, her eyes locking onto the journalist's. "Unexpected? Do you mean the collapse of a corrupt trial that was never meant to be fair from the start? Or do you mean the part where the government's puppet show fell apart in front of everyone? I'm sure the truth must have been uncomfortable for someone like you, who's been selling lies for so long."

The journalist recoiled slightly, taken aback by the directness of Christina's words. Her gaze darted briefly to the crowd, her face tight with discomfort. She shifted her weight from one foot to the other, clearly trying to maintain control of the situation. But it was too late. Christina had cornered her, and there was no escape.

Christina continued, her voice rising just enough to be heard by the few remaining spectators. "Do you even realize the damage you've done with your so-called 'journalism'? All the stories you've pushed, siding with the people who have played with Yani's life like a chess piece. You've ignored facts, manipulated the truth, and aided in perpetuating a system that thrives on injustice."

The journalist's face twitched as if each word from Christina's mouth was a blow. She opened her mouth to respond, but no words came. It was as if the shame had rendered her speechless.

Christina stepped forward, her voice low now, cutting through the air like a blade. "You've had every opportunity to report the truth, to stand for what's right. But instead, you've chosen to dance to the tune of the powerful. Tell me, how does that feel? To be so utterly complicit in the corruption you claim to report on?"

The journalist swallowed hard, her shoulders slumping in defeat. She met Christina's gaze, no longer defiant but filled with something far more dangerous, fear, fear of being exposed, of the truth she had long tried to bury coming to light.

Christina, seeing the cracks in her mask, pressed on. "You should be ashamed. You call yourself a journalist, but you've abandoned every ethical duty you swore to uphold. How many more lives will you ruin before you take responsibility for the harm you've done?"

The journalist's face flushed a deep shade of red as she took a cautious step back, her gaze shifting to her car and then to Christina. "I...I don't think this is the place for this conversation." Her voice trembled slightly now, betraying the composure she had so carefully cultivated over the years.

Christina shook her head slowly, her eyes narrowing with disdain. "No, it's the perfect place. This is when you can either face your complicity or continue running from it. Don't fool yourself into thinking you can escape accountability. Because sooner or later, the truth always catches up."

As the day wore on, the president of the Bar Association, accompanied by several members of his office, arrived at the courthouse. His arrival was purposeful; he was here to ascertain the situation firsthand and to extend official support to his colleague, David Chef, one of the leading defense attorneys in the case. It was evident that the Bar Association's involvement was not merely procedural; it was a strategic intervention aimed at asserting the integrity of the legal profession in the face of mounting irregularities.

The group proceeded directly to the office of the court president, who, visibly perturbed by the day's developments, stood up to greet them. His expression suggested that the unfolding situation had caught him off guard.

"I owe you an apology, Mr. President," the court president began, his tone apologetic but lacking conviction. "This situation has escalated beyond what I had anticipated."

With the composed demeanor of an experienced litigator, David wasted no time. "Your apology is noted but does not address the core issue. The integrity of this trial has been compromised by actions that trace their roots back to the highest echelons of power.

The alleged misconduct cannot be blamed on the actions of a few individual magistrates. It is indicative of a systemic failure that demands a much more profound remedy."

The president of the Bar Association stepped forward, his voice calm but authoritative. "The facts are irrefutable, Your Honor. If the judiciary is to maintain any semblance of credibility, this matter mustn't be treated as a case of isolated misconduct. The corruption within this institution has origins that the sanctioning of a few individuals cannot mitigate. The actions of a broader network must be addressed, not simply dismissed with token disciplinary measures."

The court president shifted uncomfortably in his seat, visibly trying to regroup, but the pressure was mounting.

"I will convene a meeting of the High Council of the Judiciary tomorrow," the court president offered, his voice slightly more defensive. "The magistrates responsible will be duly sanctioned."

However, the president of the Bar Association was unyielding. "Sanctioning a couple of judges is insufficient, Your Honor. The issue at hand is far more profound than the actions of a few rogue individuals. It is a structural issue requiring systemic reform, not just surface-level remedies."

At that moment, David, ever the advocate for his client, seized the opportunity to push for substantive change. "We demand that the trial of Ms. Yani be rescheduled with a new jury panel, one that is not compromised by the previous biases or systemic corruption that have marred this process. A fresh trial with a neutral and impartial jury is the only way forward."

The court president hesitated. His face betrayed a reluctance to engage in such a dramatic step. "I'll need to confer with Ms. Yani and her legal team in private before making any decisions."

David's gaze sharpened. "You want to meet with my client and her lawyers privately after everything that has transpired today? We are well past private conversations. The time for transparency is now."

The court president's attempt to evade the issue was palpable, but before he could respond, a journalist in the back of the room seized the moment, microphone raised. "Mr. President, what will your office do to address the situation publicly? How do you justify the proceedings so far, and what steps will be taken to restore faith in the integrity of this trial?"

The court president was caught off guard and responded with visible discomfort. "I will not be making any statements at this time," he said flatly, attempting to avoid further public scrutiny. "I must apologize, but I must return to my office to address these matters internally."

With that, the court president quickly exited the room, avoiding the press and returning to his office without offering any meaningful response. His hurried departure left the room in stunned silence, with the weight of his evasion hanging in the air.

Outside, the members of the Bar Association were joined by the defense team, whose expressions were a mixture of frustration and resolve. David exchanged a look with Estelle, who was seething with quiet anger.

"This is not over," she said under her breath. "We'll hold them accountable."

David nodded. "They can delay, hide, but they can't escape the truth."

The journalists buzzed with energy, their cameras still rolling, capturing the aftermath of a trial on the brink of collapse. Despite the court president's refusal to address the matter publicly, the voices of those advocating for justice grew louder. The Bar Association's firm stance signaled that the legal community would not stand idly by while the judicial system's integrity was compromised.

As the court president disappeared behind the heavy oak doors of his office, his hasty retreat did little to quell the rising tension within the courtroom. The murmurs of disbelief and frustration reverberated through the chamber. Outside, in the corridor, the members of the Bar Association gathered with the defense team. Their expressions were a mix of outraged disbelief and steely resolve. They had arrived at the courthouse expecting a swift resolution, but what they had witnessed had gone beyond a mere mishandling of a trial; it was an unmasking of the very foundations of justice that they had sworn to uphold.

David stood at the forefront, his posture rigid, eyes burning with the moment's weight. "This is far from over," he declared, his voice calm yet edged with a palpable frustration. "They may have momentarily evaded the public eye's scrutiny, but we will not let them conceal this under layers of bureaucracy and red tape. The facts are clear; this trial was compromised from the outset, and the world deserves to know the truth."

Estelle, standing beside him, nodded her agreement, her gaze unwavering. "We will not allow them to sweep this under the rug. Our fight is not just for Yani; it is for the very integrity of the system. We're here to make sure this never happens again."

The president of the Bar Association, a towering figure in the legal community, stepped forward, his voice steady and commanding. "If we allow this flagrant miscarriage of justice to go unchecked, it will send a dangerous message: that corruption can fester even in the halls of justice and that the courts are not a place for truth but manipulation. I will not allow that to stand."

The words were heavy, but they struck a chord with everyone present. The team shared an understanding that the battle ahead would be long, but it was a battle that had to be fought. This was no longer just about Yani's case but about something more profound: restoring trust in the justice system.

Journalists waiting on the sidelines now closed in, their cameras aimed squarely at David. They had anticipated a statement, a declaration of some kind. Still, when it became evident that the court president had no intention of offering meaningful answers, their attention shifted to the defense team.

"Mr. Chef," one reporter pressed, microphone thrust forward, "what happens now? Will you take legal action against the judge or prosecutor for misconduct?"

David met the question with a steady gaze, his answer deliberate and forceful. "The court president may believe that he can silence us by retreating behind closed doors, but I assure you, this trial was a travesty, not just a miscarriage of justice. This was the result of a corrupt system that will not go unchallenged. If powerful people believe they can bury this, they are gravely mistaken. We will make sure the world sees what transpired here today."

Another reporter, eager for more details, asked, "What do you expect from tomorrow's High Council of the Judiciary meeting? Will it lead to any meaningful changes?"

David's eyes narrowed, his tone unwavering. "We've seen this charade before. They'll likely offer token sanctions, a few symbolic actions to appease the public, but we need real accountability. We are demanding the reconstitution of this trial: a new jury, a new judge, and a new prosecutor. The judiciary must be held to the highest standards of integrity, and until that happens, this trial will remain a sham."

The reporters scrambled to capture every word, their pens flying across their notebooks, but it was clear that the answers they were seeking would not be handed to them quickly.

Inside their small conference room near the courthouse, the defense team gathered once more, joined now by several key members of the Bar Association. The mood was tense, and the conversations were rapid but focused as they strategized their next steps. There was a shared sense of purpose in the room, a clear understanding that they had not just been tasked with representing one client but with reclaiming the system itself.

"They've severely underestimated us," one of the senior lawyers from the Bar Association said, bitterness lacing his words. "If they think a few superficial apologies and internal meetings will resolve this, they are gravely mistaken."

David stood up, pacing the room with quiet intensity. "We've gathered the evidence and know the lengths they'll go to cover their tracks. But that won't stop us. We have the truth, and the world will know it. We'll take this fight beyond the courtroom. It's time to make the public see this for what it truly is. The stakes here are bigger than Yani's trial. They're about the future of justice in this country."

Estelle stepped forward, her voice low but filled with unwavering conviction. "We can't afford to back down now, David. The people are watching. If they see us stand firm, they'll support us."

Surrounded by her legal team, Yani stood still, her expression a mixture of defiance and restraint. The moment's weight hung heavily in the air as the courtroom drama spilled into the corridor. The press surged forward, cameras clicking and microphones extending toward her like a hungry swarm.

Yani, unable to speak amid the legal whirlwind, remained silent. Her defense lawyers, a tightly knit unit, formed a protective barrier around her. They knew this moment was about more than just the trial; it was about safeguarding her dignity, her rights, and their strategy for the long fight ahead.

A journalist from a prominent foreign channel stepped up, microphone in hand, intent on asking Yani a direct question. His voice cut through the low murmur of the room. "Ms. Yani, do you have any comment on today's unprecedented turn of events? The world is watching."

Before Yani could respond, Fael, one of her attorneys, stepped forward with calm authority. His voice was firm, but his manner was respectful. "Yani will not be making any statements at this time," Fael said, gazing at the journalist. "However, I will happily address your questions in her place."

The journalist, eager for answers, raised an eyebrow. "What can you tell us about the letter allegedly sent by the president to the judge? Can you confirm its authenticity and impact on the trial's fairness?"

Fael's gaze was steady, unwavering. "The existence of that letter is undeniable proof of executive interference in a case that should have been governed by the rule of law alone. A letter from the head of state to a judge about an ongoing trial violates the separation of powers. It is a clear indication of political involvement at the highest levels, and it undermines the judiciary's integrity. This is not just about one trial. It's about the very foundation of our democracy."

The journalists standing nearby felt a ripple of tension, sensing that something far more significant than Yani's case was at stake.

The foreign journalist, sensing an opportunity for further provocation, pushed back. "How can you be so sure about the contents of that letter? What if it's a misinterpretation or an exaggeration?"

Fael's voice remained composed, but there was an edge of challenge. "If you want to challenge what I've said, I suggest you visit the presidency. The letter was written at their behest, and if you doubt the facts I've laid out, they are in the best position to either confirm or deny its existence. But don't take my word for it. Go to the presidency and ask them directly."

The journalist, now slightly taken aback by Fael's directness, hesitated. "I already did," she admitted, her tone shifting. "I went to the presidency today, and no one would meet with me or provide a statement. I was turned away."

Fael gave a slight nod, as if acknowledging the apparent truth. "That's exactly what I thought. The executive hides behind their silence, hoping the truth will remain buried. But we will make sure that the public knows what's happening here. And we will ensure that the truth is not silenced by those who wield power in the shadows."

The journalist, realizing she would get no further information from Fael, nodded reluctantly and turned to another member of the press corps. But the weight of the conversation lingered, hanging in the air like a thick fog.

Behind them, the Bar Association members and other legal observers exchanged knowing glances. The silence around Yani was deliberate; her lawyers had created a clear boundary, ensuring that no further distractions would interfere with their broader mission, to expose the truth and protect Yani's rights in this complex, high-stakes fight. Amid all the chaos, Yani remained composed, and the strength of her legal team was her anchor. She could not speak to the press now, not while her lawyers worked tirelessly to unveil the corruption that had seeped into every corner of the trial. But every glance and every quiet moment were a testament to her resilience.

The wheels of justice may have temporarily stalled, but the fight was far from over. The truth was only beginning to break through the silence for Yani, her team, and the public watching.

Tension escalated in the courthouse as a long procession of black cars with tinted windows pulled up at the main entrance. The sound of tires rolling on the pavement was muted by the hum of anticipation that had enveloped the scene. A hush fell over the journalists and spectators as they realized who was arriving.

The ministers of justice, interior, defense, and finance, key figures in the government, had come to address the brewing storm. Their presence was not just a show of political might; it was clear they were here to steer the narrative, to quiet the storm that had erupted in the wake of the trial's revelations. They moved swiftly, their faces grim, the urgency of their steps revealing that their concern was more than mere curiosity; it was about control.

The journalists, eager to capture any new development, quickly shifted focus toward the main entrance, their cameras snapping furiously as the ministers exited their cars, one by one. They did not stop to engage with the media; their expressions were set in a hard line. The ministers, clad in formal attire, moved toward the large central doors of the courthouse. There was no fanfare, just a hurried, almost mechanical march toward the office of the court's president.

Inside, the ministers exchanged a few words in hushed tones, the gravity of the situation weighing on them. A minute later, they entered the office of the senior judge, where the attorney general was already waiting. The door to the office clicked shut behind them, and the silence that followed was unsettling.

In the corridor outside, David, standing with his colleagues, felt the tension thickening. The smell of polished wood and dust seemed heavier now, charged with something dark and unresolved. His attention was pulled away when a plainclothes policeman approached him, his face stoic.

"You're expected in the office of the senior judge," the officer said, his voice low, almost conspiratorial.

David's jaw tightened. He turned to his team, his gaze scanning their faces. The entire legal team was already on edge. He relayed the message to them, but the answer came swiftly and decisively.

"We won't speak behind closed doors," Estelle declared firmly, her voice carrying weight. "If they want to talk, it will be in public. They're mistaken if they think they can settle this mess secretly."

The other lawyers nodded in agreement, their resolve hardening. They had already seen how the system operated in the shadows; it was time to drag the darkness into the light.

The president of the Bar Association, standing beside them, voiced his support, his tone unyielding. "This is a matter of public trust. If there is any talk to be had, it should be in front of the people. They have a right to know what's going on behind the scenes. If we go into that office now, it will only serve to protect the guilty. We'll stand by our decision, no backroom deals."

David's lips pressed into a thin line. He understood the stakes, Yani's future and the integrity of the entire judicial system were on the line. A private discussion with the government ministers would only legitimize their efforts to cover up the corruption. "We'll go in, but not quietly," David said, his voice low but determined. "Let's show them we're not afraid to expose the truth, no matter who's in that room. This is about more than Yani now. It's about the future of justice itself."

The members of the Bar Association, standing alongside the defense team, echoed their agreement. It was no longer about defending a single client but ensuring the entire system could be held accountable. Their support gave David the strength to take the next step with unwavering confidence.

As the team moved toward the senior judge's office, they were surrounded by an air of defiance. They were no longer merely participants in a trial; they had become agents of change, determined to hold the powerful accountable, no matter the cost.

Sensing the shift in momentum, the reporters crowded behind the team, eager to capture every word and gesture. The courthouse had become a battlefield, with public opinion as the ultimate prize.

David stopped briefly as he reached the office door, turning to his team and the journalists who had gathered around them. He took a deep breath.

"Let them hear us," he said, his voice steady but filled with resolve. "We'll speak the truth, no matter who tries to silence us."

And with that, they entered the room, the door swinging open, the specter of justice hanging heavy in the air as the government and the legal team prepared to face each other under the public eye's scrutiny.

The tension in the room reached a fever pitch. The presence of David, his legal team, the Bar Association, and the journalists had turned the room into an arena, and the ministers sitting in solemn discussion were now caught in the glare of the public eye.

When the lawyers and journalists filed into the room, the ministers sprang to their feet in unison, their faces painted with feigned surprise and outrage. Their performances were so transparent that even the most casual observer would have noticed the deceit. Still, they were playing a game, hoping to maintain the illusion of righteous indignation in front of the press.

The minister of justice, his face flushed and his hands slightly trembling, was the first to speak. His voice rang with feigned moral outrage.

"This situation, this corruption, is appalling," he said, his voice rising with manufactured emotion. "We, as a government, are deeply disturbed by the news. I just left a meeting with the president of the Republic, and we are shocked by the corruption within the judicial system. The president has expressed his disbelief and outrage and wants the perpetrators punished. I can assure you justice will be done. We are already moving to sanction those responsible."

The assembled ministers nodded in hollow agreement, their faces a mix of strained concern and barely concealed panic. They were trying to buy time, deflecting attention away from the real issue, their involvement in this scandal.

However, before they could continue their charade, an independent news agency journalist raised his hand, cutting through the drama with a pointed question.

"Minister," he began, his voice steady, "can you confirm if the letter sent to the judge was written by the president of the Republic or anyone within the presidency?"

The room went silent. The minister of justice froze, his eyes widening as he tried to gather himself. He had not expected the question, and for a moment, the carefully constructed layers of his defense crumbled. Sweat beaded on his forehead as he stammered, searching for words.

"W-well, no," he muttered, his voice faltering. "The letter was...it was not directly from the president. It was an internal memorandum from the justice ministry, part of routine procedures to ensure—"

Another journalist, sensing the lie, jumped in. "So you're telling us that the president was only informed about this letter this afternoon? The letter was written this morning? Are you implying that the president did not know of it beforehand?"

The minister of justice's face drained of color as he realized he was being cornered. His mouth opened, but no words came out. He tried to recover, his hands shaking as he fumbled with his notes. His earlier bravado was now completely shattered.

"You're twisting my words!" he shouted, his voice cracking with frustration. "The president was informed. He didn't know the full extent of the issue until later!"

But the journalist was unrelenting. "So the president, your boss, didn't know about the letter this morning when it was drafted? And now you're telling us he was shocked this afternoon? You'll have to excuse me, Minister, but you're not making sense."

The minister of justice's face flushed red with rage. His teeth clenched as his eyes narrowed into a glare. "You have no right to question me like that! I'll have you—" His words were abruptly cut off as a hiss of disapproval rippled through the room.

The crowd, journalists, lawyers, and even a few lingering bystanders, began to murmur in anger. The tension escalated quickly, and it wasn't just the press or the public reacting. Several lawyers, their patience stretched to the breaking point, stepped forward, their voices rising.

"Who are you trying to fool, Minister?" one of the senior lawyers from the Bar Association snapped. "This is a blatant cover-up, and you think we'll let you get away with it?"

Another lawyer, red with indignation, muttered, "You think you can deceive us like this? The people can see through your lies."

In an instant, the mood in the room shifted from pressing concern to outright fury. The ministers, who had been pretending to be in control, were now visibly uncomfortable. The minister of justice, flustered and angry, raised his voice to regain command.

"You need to watch how you speak to me!" he barked. "We're not here to be lectured by—"

Before he could finish, another journalist cut him off, laughing bitterly. "Oh, so now you're threatening the media? I suppose the president's surprise letter was a coincidence too?"

The ministers, now visibly shaken, exchanged uneasy glances. Their confidence was slipping away as the room filled with the rising sound of distrust and disapproval. The situation was quickly spiraling out of their control.

The senior judge, silently observing from the sidelines, finally stood and tried to regain some semblance of order.

The room vibrated with collective energy, and an overwhelming sense of disillusionment and righteous anger thickened. The once influential figures, the ministers, now appeared more like frail actors caught in a script they didn't write, stammering through lines they could no longer convincingly perform.

David, seeing the scene unfold with growing determination, stepped forward. His voice was calm but rang with undeniable resolve as he addressed the ministers and the crowd. "Let's not be distracted by their games," he said, looking directly at the minister of justice. "We all know the truth now. The president's letter was part of a far-reaching strategy, and this trial is merely a symptom of a deeper sickness. We won't let you spin it into a few bad apples in the judicial system."

The crowd stirred in agreement, their murmurs of approval swelling into louder chants. Journalists held their microphones higher, determined to capture every word, every gesture.

"I suggest," David continued, gazing at the senior judge, "that you stop pretending this can be cleaned up with a few superficial sanctions. We demand accountability at the highest level."

The senior judge seemed to shrink in stature momentarily, his previously unflappable facade cracking as he glanced at the ministers. They were in no better shape. The minister of justice clenched his jaw tightly, visibly struggling to maintain his composure. The game he'd been playing was no longer an option.

Before he could respond, the minister of defense, still clutching his phone, spoke up, his voice low but filled with urgency. "We'll handle this. Give us a few more moments." He gestured toward the plainclothes policemen, who had slowly started moving toward the back of the room, subtly positioning themselves near the exits. The tension in the room was palpable as everyone became aware of their presence.

The air seemed to freeze as the crowd quieted for a beat, and then, in a voice sharp with suspicion, one of the journalists asked the obvious question. "Is this how you plan to resolve it, Minister? By threatening the press, the lawyers, and the people demanding justice?"

The minister of defense straightened, clearly irritated by the public exposure of his intentions. "You don't understand what you're dealing with," he snapped, his voice low but filled with an edge that cut through the room. "Sometimes, the truth is too dangerous to let out. But we will make sure this situation is resolved."

His words hung in the air like a warning. The room erupted in disbelief. A chorus of voices, from lawyers, activists, and even the journalists, filled the room, protesting his words.

"This is exactly the kind of corruption we're fighting against!" shouted a lawyer from the Bar Association. "You're talking about silencing the truth!"

The ministers, already looking out of their depth, tried to regain their composure but struggled. Their courage was fading as the crowd rallied behind David's words.

In a desperate attempt to control the narrative, the minister of justice raised his hands in a defensive gesture. "I understand the anger here, but the president wants us to focus on resolving this problem. The judiciary has its issues, but we can't just tear everything down."

At that moment, another journalist interrupted him with a sharp question. "Are you saying the president is unaware of what has happened in his courts? That his letter was a reaction to a surprise?"

The minister's face flushed deeper, his earlier bravado now completely gone. He stammered but couldn't form a coherent sentence. The senior judge stepped forward, attempting to control the situation, but the crowd's restlessness was getting harder to contain.

Then a disturbing sound broke the tense atmosphere: the unmistakable hum of heavy machinery, the sound of engines revving, and the low rumble of armored vehicles. The minister of defense, watching the crowd nervously, stiffened when he heard the sound.

"Let them through," the minister of defense muttered under his breath, his eyes narrowing as he turned back to the senior judge.

The crowd shifted uneasily as the heavy doors at the back of the room creaked open, and a line of armored vehicles rolled into view. The unmistakable shape of battering rams appeared in the rear of the courtroom. The very sight of them was enough to send a ripple of fear through the crowd.

Sensing the shift in dynamics, the senior judge raised his hands again to calm everyone down. "Please…please, let's take a step back," he pleaded. "There is no need for any further escalation."

But his voice was drowned out by the growing clamor. The crowd's frustration and the lawyers' collective fury reached a boiling point. Someone from the back shouted, "We won't be intimidated!"

CHAPTER 8

As the clock struck 6:00 p.m., the oppressive atmosphere in the courthouse seemed to thicken, more tangible than ever. The ministers, weighed down by the crisis they had initiated, exchanged nervous glances as they shuffled in uneasy circles.

Journalists clutched their microphones with tense fingers, their cameras still rolling, eyes darting from one politician to another, waiting for the next shift in the drama.

Lawyers, their expressions a mixture of defiance and determination, lingered around the room, watching the unfolding scene. At the same time, outside the courthouse, the hum of armored vehicles and the unmistakable presence of the military loomed large, ready and waiting for any signal that might give them orders to intervene.

In this charged environment, David caught Fael's eye. There was no need for words. He leaned in, whispering something quick but decisive in his colleague's ear. Fael, ever the tactician, nodded almost imperceptibly and immediately motioned for Yani, the journalists, and their team to gather.

The room shifted slightly as the ministers moved toward the Bar Association president, clearly panicked and trying to control the situation.

"David, you can't possibly think this is the right time for that," one of the ministers of finance protested, his voice tinged with anxiety and authority. "There are still negotiations. Let's talk privately. Let's work this out."

But David stood firm, his eyes never leaving Yani as she moved toward the press. With a calm smile, she took her place at the front, and the room, a mixture of confusion and anticipation, slowly quieted.

With a nod of approval from the crowd, journalists settled in, ready for the scoop they knew would shape history. Yani stepped up, the camera lights flashing in her face, yet her composure never wavered.

"Good evening," Yani began, her voice steady but resonant with a quiet power. "I am Detective Yani, and I've worked for the judicial police for years. You might be asking why a detective is standing here today, speaking not just as a witness but as someone who's lived through this injustice. Let me explain."

The room leaned forward, the buzz of anticipation palpable. Even the ministers exchanged glances, their unease evident as Yani's voice echoed through the court.

"I've been a detective for years. I've worked cases of all sorts: murder, fraud, corruption. But you wouldn't realize how deep the rot goes until you investigate the system itself."

Her gaze flickered across the room, meeting the eyes of the journalists, lawyers, and even the ministers who now looked on with growing concern.

She paused briefly, letting her words sink in before continuing.

"It all started with a small file," she said, her voice dropping slightly. "A petty theft case. Hardly the kind of thing that gets a detective excited, right? But as I started to dig, I found something that made me question everything I had ever believed about the system I worked for."

The crowd stirred, murmurs of disbelief and curiosity rippling through the room. Fael, standing just behind her, smiled faintly. He knew where this was going.

Yani paused for dramatic effect, allowing the silence in the room to grow thick. "What I found wasn't just petty theft. It was a web of corruption. Forgery, money laundering, and far more sinister crimes were hidden in plain sight behind layers of bureaucracy. And the deeper I dug, the more I uncovered."

The ministers, now visibly uncomfortable, exchanged hurried words among themselves. But it was too late. The press had already latched onto Yani's every word.

Yani continued, her voice more determined now, carrying the weight of her knowledge. "The file I was given wasn't just a small-time burglary case. It was part of a bigger investigation, a massive scam involving some of the most powerful people in the country. And I wasn't the only one to discover it."

Her tone shifted, turning a bit darker. "It wasn't until another colleague, one who had no idea what they were getting into, found a second file. That file revealed even darker truths. What we had uncovered went far beyond anything the police or the court system had ever imagined. It was the tip of the iceberg."

She looked around the room, the audience hanging on her every word.

"I knew that the system would fight back. I knew they would bury it. So when I tried to push further, that's when the attacks began. Threats. Intimidation. Even physical harassment. But it didn't stop there. People I worked with, people I trusted, started disappearing. Important documents went missing."

Yani took a deep breath, her gaze sweeping across the crowd, noting how even the ministers were now visibly sweating. They couldn't ignore the truth now.

"I was targeted, ostracized, and ultimately set up to take the fall for something that was never my doing. But now, I have a voice, and this trial."

As the military officer raised his hand, signaling his men to advance, the tension in the courtroom reached its breaking point. The boots echoed against the marble floors, creating a jarring rhythm that almost drowned out the crowd's breath.

Journalists scrambled to adjust their cameras, eager not to miss a moment of the unfolding drama.

But Yani, unwavering, remained at the center of the press conference, her eyes locked on the officer as he approached. Her posture was strong, as though she had already faced worse threats than these soldiers. She wasn't just speaking for herself anymore; she was speaking for everyone who had ever been silenced or ignored by a broken system.

David stepped forward, placing a firm hand on the shoulder of the military officer who had spoken. His voice rang out, calm but resolute, as if challenging the officer and everything the officer represented. "We are not moving, not until the truth has been acknowledged."

The officer's gaze hardened, but he didn't immediately respond. Instead, he motioned for a couple of his men to approach the group. The lawyers stiffened, ready to protect their client at any cost, their hands inching toward the documents they had spent months collecting.

The standoff felt like it lasted forever, and the courtroom was filled with the tension of an impending storm. But the crowd outside added to the weight of the moment. Through the courtroom's high windows, David could see activists, ordinary citizens, and students gathered in the square, holding signs and chanting, their faces a mixture of hope and anger. They were ready to fight, not only for Yani but also for the future of the country and its justice system.

The ministers, whose faces were now pale from embarrassment and panic, exchanged anxious glances, realizing they were on the verge of losing complete control of the narrative. The courtroom had begun to feel more like a public arena than a place of law. Just as the tension seemed to peak, one minister stepped forward, raising his hands in an attempt to regain some semblance of authority.

"Enough!" The minister of the interior quickly added, 'You're right, David, we need dialogue. This will not help. We can't solve anything by escalating the situation." His eyes darted from the lawyers to the soldiers and then to the crowd, pressing against the courthouse's heavy wooden doors. "We need equity, not chaos."

The minister agreed. "You're right, David, we need dialogue."

But the reaction was swift. Emboldened by the events unfolding, a journalist raised his microphone toward the minister. "Minister, you were seen entering the office of the senior judge today. Can you explain why the president of the Republic sent a letter to the judge, asking for intervention in this trial? Is that part of the dialogue you speak of?"

The minister faltered. His lips tightened, and he looked like he might implode momentarily. The earlier panicked avoidance of the subject gave way to an outright lie. "I…I don't know exactly what to say about that. I presume the letter… Frankly, the president was unaware of its contents."

The journalist didn't have it. "So the president of the Republic wasn't involved at all? You're saying this letter didn't come from him or anyone in his office?"

The minister's eyes narrowed, his hands clenched, and he looked truly and deeply cornered for the first time. "I don't—"

Before he could continue, the same journalist pressed harder, his voice sharper now. The letter from the president wasn't sent until this morning, Minister. Are you claiming you didn't know until this afternoon?"

"I…I don't have to answer to you," the minister snapped, his voice rising, his desperation evident. "This is a state matter. We're doing our best to address this situation, and we don't need the press turning it into a spectacle!"

At that point, the crowd erupted in dismay, with lawyers, journalists, and even soldiers shaking their heads at the minister's transparent attempt to evade responsibility. Sensing the momentum shift, Yani lifted her voice, her voice now clear, calm, and piercing.

"We know the truth," she said, her gaze cutting across the room. "And the truth doesn't change, no matter how many lies you tell. I'm not here to play politics. I'm here to fight for justice. And whether you like it or not, the world is watching."

The ministers glanced at one another, exchanging uncertain looks. The facade of control they had desperately clung to was unraveling before their eyes, and they knew it.

As if on cue, the senior judge, who had been silent until now, stood from his seat. His eyes were bloodshot.

The air thickened with the weight of everything left unsaid. The ministers were visibly shaking, each caught between the pressure to maintain their power and the undeniable truth now spiraling out of their control. Outside, the presence of military vehicles and armed guards had become impossible to ignore, as if the courthouse itself were under siege. But inside, the real battle still took place in words.

It was no longer about the courtroom but survival in the court of public opinion.

The room fell into a heavy silence, broken only by the sound of a prominent journalist who had stepped forward from the back of the crowd. Known for her sharp investigative reporting, she was a figure who had long been a thorn in the side of those in power. Her reputation for asking the hard questions earned her both respect and disdain, and today, she was more than ready to add another chapter to her legacy.

With her microphone raised, she looked toward the ministers standing before the group, her voice cutting through the tension like a blade.

"Ministers," she said, her tone calm but with an edge that made the room fall even quieter, "given the mounting evidence of corruption that has come to light today, there are still many questions about the involvement of the highest levels of government in this entire debacle. But I want to ask you one straightforward question. Is the presidency of this country actively encouraging this state of corruption?"

Her words hung in the air like an undeniable accusation that could not be ignored. The crowd shifted, some leaning in to hear more clearly while others held their breath, waiting for the response that would shape the day's outcome. The question was both simple and profound, daring in its directness.

The ministers exchanged quick, nervous glances, clearly unprepared for such a pointed challenge. Their attempts to maintain their composure faltered. The minister of justice, who had already been struggling to keep his stance, stepped forward, his face a mask of feigned indignation.

"No," he said quickly, his voice trembling slightly. "The presidency is committed to fighting corruption, just as we are. We are doing everything we can to address this issue, and any suggestion that the government is somehow involved in fostering corruption is completely false."

The journalist didn't flinch. She held his gaze, her eyes burning with the hunger for the truth.

"Then why," she asked, her voice rising now, "did the president of the Republic send a letter to the senior judge in this very case, pressuring her to intervene? How do you explain that if the presidency is so committed to the rule of law and transparency?"

For a moment, the minister of justice was taken aback. His lips parted as if to speak, but no words came out. His earlier bravado had vanished, leaving only a thin veneer of defensiveness.

The minister of the interior, trying to salvage the situation, quickly stepped in. "What the president has done, if indeed he was involved, was only in response to concerns brought to him by the judicial system itself. It's a matter of ensuring fairness and ensuring that—"

But before he could finish, another journalist, a younger reporter who had been following the case closely, stood up and interrupted him.

"Minister," she said cynically, "are we to believe that the president only just heard about the letter this afternoon? Was he unaware of a letter written this morning that specifically addressed the judge in this trial? How do you explain that timeline? Are you seriously suggesting that the presidency was not involved until the last minute?"

The minister froze, and the entire room seemed to hold its breath. Heavy with the stench of lies and half-truths, the room buzzed with the energy of the journalist's bold question. It was as if the minister of justice could feel the walls closing in, the truth slowly suffocating his carefully crafted narrative.

"I...I..." he stammered, trying to collect his thoughts. "This situation is..."

His voice trailed off as the room erupted. Journalists started shouting questions, bombarding the ministers with inquiries about the president's involvement, the letter, and the corruption that no one seemed willing to admit had been stitched together long before the trial and had grown into a web of deception.

Then the minister of finance arrived late. He had been silent until this point but finally spoke up, his voice low and desperate. "We're not here to discuss the presidency or his actions. We are here to address the issues and ensure justice is served."

But the crowd wasn't having it. Their patience was running thin, and the journalists were relentless. The lawyers, David, Estelle, Fael, and the others, stood firm, their faces marked with the resolve of people who had already made up their minds about the truth.

The air was thick with tension, a weight steadily building as the ministers tried to regain some semblance of control over the escalating situation. But just as they began to shuffle their feet in uneasy silence, a new sound broke through the room, an endless chorus of phone notifications.

Lawyers, journalists, activists, and even a few judges present all had their phones buzzing incessantly. Their faces, already strained from the earlier confrontations, were now etched with something more: shock.

One by one, they answered their phones, quickly muttering words of disbelief, their eyes widening as they listened. The message had gone viral. It wasn't just whispers anymore; it was a declaration, an undeniable storm.

The audio, released just moments earlier, had already started making the rounds, and it was clear why the room had gone silent. An individual who had remained in the shadows until now had confirmed the authenticity of the explosive secret document linked to the president. In a cold, measured tone, the speaker confirmed the existence of the letter sent to the senior judge, and perhaps more damning, he claimed to hold state secrets implicating some of the most influential figures in the republic.

The recording continued, each word heavy with the gravity of what had been set in motion. The individual promised the full release of the documents at 8:00 p.m. sharp. He gave the names of all those involved and a list of the country's most influential figures, the ones who had been complicit in the corruption, manipulation, and crimes that had been covered up for so long.

As the journalists, activists, and lawyers processed this information, a journalist at the front, microphone in hand, seized the moment. Her voice rang out, cutting through the murmurs of disbelief.

"Ministers," she called, her tone razor-sharp. "Given this startling new revelation, how do you respond to the fact that a person, clearly in possession of sensitive state documents, has just announced that they will publish the entire file tonight at 8:00 p.m.? With the identities of all those involved? Does this not implicate the highest levels of government, including your offices? What's your take on this?"

Her words hung in the air, and the ministers looked around, panic evident on their faces. It was all closing in on them. The minister of justice took a hesitant step forward, opening his mouth as if he were thinking of saying something, but no sound came out. The minister of defense, who had been keeping a low profile, rubbed his temples, trying to process the implications of what was unfolding.

The minister of finance glanced around the room, eyes darting from one person to the next, looking for an escape, a way out of the mounting chaos. But there was nowhere to run.

The minister of justice finally spoke, his voice faltering. "This is a serious matter we must look into immediately. I—"

But before he could finish, another journalist interrupted, her voice dripping with disbelief. "Aren't you being a bit too late to act? The president has known about this for hours, and you only seem to be reacting now, in the middle of an escalating crisis."

The room grew quiet. The ministers, unable to respond with any authority, exchanged glances, panic written on their faces. Their efforts to control the narrative had failed utterly. The story had already spun beyond their reach, unraveling before their eyes.

A few seconds later, the ministers did their best. They retreated.

In a flurry of movement, they left the room. Defeated, they hurried through the side doors, disappearing into their armored vehicles, their black-tinted windows concealing their panic-stricken expressions. As they drove away, there was no longer any pretense of power, and there were no more speeches to the crowd. They were out of sight, and with their departure, the illusion of authority crumbled, leaving behind nothing but a room full of people who saw through the facade.

In their wake, the room was filled with rushing feet and murmurs of disbelief. The journalists, emboldened by the new evidence, began to speak in rapid, hushed tones. They prepared their articles, eager to capture every detail of the unfolding story.

As the minutes passed, it became clear that the battle for the country's justice had shifted irrevocably. This was no longer just about one trial. It was about the entire system, a system that had been propped up by lies, deception, and corruption at the highest levels for too long.

As the ministers sped away, powerless to stop the tidal wave of truth unleashed, everyone knew that the 8:00 p.m. broadcast was coming and, with it, the ultimate reckoning.

It was no longer just a question of politics; it was a question of accountability. And the people, the journalists, and the lawyers would not rest until they had seen it.

As the last of the ministers disappeared behind the heavy gates of the courthouse, a palpable shift took place in the room. The journalists, now emboldened by the events, gathered around Yani and her legal team, their cameras flashing rapidly as they captured the faces of the courageous figures who had helped bring this fight to light.

David, Estelle, Fael, and the rest of the team were still standing, their eyes a mixture of exhaustion and triumph. Their stoic expressions softened as the Bar Association members, journalists, and even some activists approached them, offering their congratulations.

A prominent member of the bar, her voice steady but filled with admiration, stepped forward. "What you've done today is nothing **short of** remarkable," she said, shaking David's hand firmly. "You've given us hope…hope that justice, no matter how deeply buried, can still see the light of day."

The others nodded in agreement, their words more genuine than scripted praise. The journalists, still carrying the weight of the breaking news, were no longer hostile. They had seen the injustice unfold, and now they saw the courage of those who had stood up to it. Their words of encouragement came fast and thick.

"Yani," one journalist said, approaching her with respect. "You've shown us all what it means to stand up, even when the odds are stacked against you. Thank you for being a beacon in all this."

Usually reserved and humble, Yani allowed a small smile to escape her lips. She nodded, looking at her lawyers, who had fought by her side. She was acutely aware that their courage had come at a cost, not just for her, but for all of them. But in this moment, their shared struggle had brought them closer, united in a common cause.

As the conversations continued, filled with words of appreciation, the crowd outside the courtroom began to swell. Word had spread, and the people waiting for the storm to break now stood in solidarity with Yani and her team. Their applause and cheers echoed through the corridors, a testament to the widespread support for the truth that had been exposed.

But time was running out. The clock was ticking toward 7:00 p.m.

The atmosphere among the lawyers and journalists shifted from celebration to anticipation as they knew the test lay ahead. David gathered his team one last time, his face set with determination.

"We've fought this battle, but now we must prepare for what's coming. We don't know who this individual is or what the full extent of their revelations will be. But when those documents drop, everything will change."

The others nodded grimly, the weight of the coming hour sinking in.

As the press began to disperse, many to file their reports or prepare for the oncoming broadcast, the lawyers and their team exited the courthouse. The Bar Association members stayed behind a little longer, conferring among themselves, no doubt already discussing how they would proceed with the fallout from the day's events.

Yani, surrounded by her lawyers, left the courthouse and hurried home. The streets, usually filled with the hum of daily life, seemed quieter now. People were in their homes, glued to their televisions, phones, and computers, preparing for the historic moment ahead.

David and the others rushed to their homes as well. The streets felt heavier as they walked, each of them no longer just concerned with their client's fate but with the fate of the entire nation. The publication of the secret documents was more than just an exposure of corruption; it was a reckoning.

By 7:30 p.m., the city was alive with whispers, every conversation turning to the documents about to be revealed. People gathered in front of TVs, some in cafés, others in living rooms, all waiting for the clock to strike the hour.

At 8:00 p.m. sharp, every screen, every phone, and every device was suddenly alive with a buzz of activity as the anonymous individual released the documents to the public.

The broadcasts began, and across the nation, the contents of the documents were revealed in their full, damning detail. The names of the most influential figures in the government and judiciary were laid bare, and their connections to corruption, bribery, and political manipulation were exposed in black and white.

The people watched silently, then began to murmur, their disbelief growing as the truth unfolded. What had once been whispered about in corners and shadows was now indisputable.

The same thought reverberated inside every street and every home: "These change everything."

Meanwhile, Yani and her legal team sat in their homes, eyes fixed on their screens, as they too watched the broadcast unfold. There was no celebrating until the full weight of what they had set in motion was fully realized. But for the first time in a long time, Yani felt a flicker of something she hadn't allowed herself in years: hope.

As the documents continued to circulate, the weight of truth settled over the nation like a heavy, unyielding fog. The information laid bare in those pages was staggering, undeniable in its implications. The names of ministers, judges, and high-ranking officials were exposed, and the network of corruption spread throughout the nation's government and judiciary. It was no longer a matter of isolated scandals or rumors; it was a systemic disease that infected the very core of the country's institutions.

By 8:30 p.m., the mood in the streets had shifted from quiet anticipation to something darker, more charged. Phones buzzed, social media lit up, and TV stations broadcast the breaking news in a loop. The revelations were not just shocking; they were historic. The walls of government offices and courts no longer protected the names of the powerful. The public had been handed the raw, unvarnished truth.

As the evening wore on, it became clear that the nation's collective conscience had been shaken. People from all walks of life, ordinary citizens, workers, students, activists, and even some politicians, began flooding the streets in groups. Their voices rose in a chorus of discontent.

The message was clear: resignation.

Shouts of "Down with corruption!" and "Resign now!" echoed through the streets. Protests erupted spontaneously in major cities and towns, fueled by the anger and betrayal that had been simmering beneath the surface for so long. Crowds gathered in front of government buildings, at the steps of the presidential palace, and outside the homes of the most powerful figures named in the documents. The people demanded accountability, and their voices rang out like a tide that could not be stopped.

In the capital, thousands of citizens poured into the main square in front of the presidential palace, waving signs and chanting. Their faces displayed a mix of fury and determination. The crowd swelled with each passing minute, the pressure mounting on the government.

"The president must go!" some shouted.

"The entire government must resign!" others echoed, their voices growing louder, the sound rippling through the streets like a rising storm.

The atmosphere was electric in the media room, where journalists reported on the unfolding crisis. A few journalists had already begun calling for the resignation of the president, the prime minister, and the entire cabinet. The newsroom buzzed with activity as reporters and editors scrambled to follow the growing chaos outside, their screens alive with updates, live feeds, and comments from both citizens and politicians.

Amid it all, the Bar Association, still surrounded by the media and various activists, continued to stand firm in its commitment to justice. They had spent hours fielding questions, answering inquiries, and offering statements to the press. But now, their faces were etched with grim satisfaction and determination.

Standing alongside his team, David saw the crowd growing larger by the minute. Yani, surrounded by her lawyers, looked out at the protests from the window of the small conference room they had retreated to. The sight of the masses, a mix of citizens, journalists, and activists, marching in solidarity was overwhelming.

The sense of unity and purpose was palpable. This wasn't just about Yani anymore; it was about a nation reclaiming its dignity, its trust in the justice system, and its future.

The public was no longer just demanding the resignation of the president or the prime minister; they were demanding a complete reckoning with the corrupt system that had held sway for far too long.

Amid the tumult, the military remained on high alert, with soldiers seen lining the streets and standing guard near government buildings. But despite their presence, the streets were not filled with fear. Instead, there was an air of defiance, a determination to see this through, come what may. The people had taken back their voice and used it to demand change.

As midnight approached, Yani's name became a rallying cry. It was no longer just the lawyers or journalists who spoke her name; every citizen saw the symbol of the struggle against corruption in her. The government had underestimated the people's resolve, and now, the weight of their collective will was on full display.

In the stillness of the night, with only the faint hum of the protests in the distance, David turned to Yani, a rare smile crossing his lips.

"We did it," he said softly, the satisfaction in his voice barely masking the exhaustion.

Yani didn't smile back. Her eyes were fixed on the scene unfolding outside. "This is just the beginning," she replied, her voice steady. "The fight isn't over. Not until every last one of them is held accountable."

And in that moment, as the public's fury reverberated through the streets, it was clear to everyone that a new chapter had begun.

Those documents were a devastating collection of truths that shattered the illusion of justice and exposed the deep-rooted corruption festering within the government. As each page was scrutinized, a chilling pattern of crimes emerged, intertwining the highest echelons of power with a web of deceit, manipulation, and criminality.

Here are some of the most heinous and disturbing crimes found within the documents:

The documents revealed systematic embezzlement of public funds allocated for critical infrastructure projects. Senior government officials, including ministers of finance and justice, had been redirecting billions into offshore accounts under the guise of construction contracts and foreign aid.

Falsified invoices and fake bids were created to divert money meant for constructing schools, hospitals, and roads into private bank accounts, most notably those belonging to high-ranking judges and politicians.

One specific example highlighted the justice minister orchestrating the diversion of funds allocated for a national digital justice system into a slush fund for personal use. The project had been delayed for over a decade despite the public being told it was in progress.

Several judges were implicated in accepting bribes to alter verdicts. The documents included evidence of secret meetings between ministers and judges, with payoffs made in exchange for favorable rulings in sensitive cases, especially those involving corporations and political allies.

The most damning case involved a prominent corporation that had illegally polluted the country's largest river for years, causing an environmental disaster. A judge, influenced by a bribe of millions, deliberately delayed hearings, allowing the company to continue operations unchecked for another five years.

Another instance involved a high-profile political figure accused of embezzling funds from the national treasury. Despite overwhelming evidence, a court ruling orchestrated through bribery saw the charges against him dropped. The documents showed detailed records of the payoff made to the presiding judge.

Several key figures in the intelligence community and the ministry of the interior had been running an illegal surveillance program, tapping phones and monitoring internet communications of political dissidents, journalists, and activists.

The documents revealed a vast network of interceptions, including emails, phone calls, and encrypted messages from opposition leaders, used to gather dirt on opponents and silence critics.

The president and his inner circle were found to have been directly involved in these illegal surveillance activities. They had authorized the spying in exchange for information used to blackmail political rivals and journalists. Several opposition politicians had been falsely accused and imprisoned based on fabricated evidence generated from these illegally gathered materials.

The documents contained a series of secret reports from human rights organizations documenting the brutal treatment of prisoners of conscience in the country's detention centers. Some individuals had been imprisoned for speaking out against government corruption or challenging the regime.

The reports detailed torture techniques used in state-run facilities, including waterboarding, electroshock, and psychological abuse. There was direct evidence of government officials personally overseeing the torture of political prisoners to extract confessions and force false testimonies.

The involvement of high-ranking officials in this abuse was irrefutable. The documents included photographs, official records, and eyewitness accounts corroborating the widespread use of state violence to suppress political opposition.

One of the more shocking revelations was the involvement of the ministry of defense in illegal arms deals with foreign governments and militant groups. The documents showed illicit shipments of weapons to conflict zones in neighboring countries in violation of international law and sanctions.

These deals were facilitated by high-ranking military officers who received kickbacks for allowing the illegal transfers. The military used its assets to facilitate these transactions while manipulating the country's military budget to cover the missing funds and weapons.

The defense minister was found to have signed multiple confidential contracts authorizing the transfer of high-grade weaponry to a paramilitary group with known ties to terrorist organizations. This not only endangered national security but also violated numerous international treaties.

The mood in the streets and in every corner of the city was electric, with the anticipation that only a moment of monumental change could bring. The revelations from the secret documents had ignited something in the people, something powerful, a collective recognition that the system they had long trusted had betrayed them at every turn.

Thousands of voices filled the air, united in their demand for accountability. There were calls for resignations and the immediate removal of those responsible for the catastrophic erosion of justice. It was no longer a protest but a movement.

As the evening stretched on, the public outcry intensified. People gathered in squares, outside government buildings, and even in the quiet corners of cafés, speaking in urgent whispers or shouting with raw emotion. News of the corrupt government had spread like wildfire, sparking a firestorm of discussions, debates, and impassioned pleas for reform.

CHAPTER 9

The following day broke with an eerie calm, as if the city held its breath after the previous day's chaos. The sun rose slowly, casting a soft orange glow across the city, painting the buildings with a temporary veneer of warmth. However, despite the promise of a new day, the air felt thick with tension and uncertainty. Once full of life, the streets seemed empty, as if the entire city had collectively paused, unsure of what to do next.

The once-bustling avenues, lined with vendors, commuters, and cars honking impatiently, now appeared almost deserted. The usual hum of urban life was subdued, replaced by a quiet, nearly suffocating air. Only a few stragglers walked along the streets, their faces tired and worn, as if the weight of the previous night's revelations had yet to lift. The occasional clink of metal or a distant siren broke the silence, but everything felt like it was on the edge of something far more significant.

Though clear, the sky above seemed less vibrant, as if it had taken on the gloom of the day's events. Even the trees lining the sidewalks swayed less today, their leaves more still than usual.

People had stayed up through the night, glued to their screens, reading the latest revelations from the media. News kiosks on street corners displayed the headlines that would soon reverberate through every home. Even the birds that had earlier chirped from their perches seemed quiet.

Inside Yani's modest apartment, the atmosphere was one of subdued reflection. The condo, typically cluttered with papers, files, and the occasional cup of half-drunk coffee, had a stark sense of emptiness today. Yani sat by the window, staring out into the city, her expression a mix of exhaustion and determination. The soft morning light filtered through the drawn blinds, but she didn't reach for the phone or the papers on the small coffee table before her. It was as though she was trying to give herself a moment of silence, to take in the enormity of what had happened, what she had been part of.

Today, her apartment was not a place of celebration. It was a space for quiet reflection on what had been exposed and, more importantly, what might still come.

The phone buzzed with constant notifications, but she ignored it for now. David, Estelle, Fael, Carlos, Ari, and Christina would all be feeling the same pressure, but right now, it felt like she needed to stand still in the face of everything swirling around her.

In sharp contrast, David's apartment was an overwhelming mix of action and strategy. His mind, usually sharp and calculating, had yet to slow from the whirlwind of events. Legal documents were scattered across the desk, some hastily put aside, others highlighted and marked with red ink; there was no time to be meticulous today. He had tried to sleep, but his rest had been fragmented, his mind too occupied with what was to come.

He hadn't slept long, and when the sunlight crept through the curtains, he knew it was time to act. His phone rang off the hook, the vibrations constant against the wooden desk. Messages from colleagues, the Bar Association, journalists, and activists filled the screen. Every one of them asked questions, offered support, or demanded action.

David ran a hand through his hair, exhaustion painting his face. It was time to focus. The next move had to be precise and powerful.

Estelle stood by the kitchen counter in her apartment, brewing a fresh pot of coffee. The house was quiet, too quiet. She gazed out the window, watching a few people walk by, their faces reflecting the same uncertainty she felt inside. She hadn't slept well either. The weight of the past few days had been too heavy, the tension building like a storm on the horizon.

Her phone buzzed incessantly on the counter. She knew what the messages contained, the same questions and demands: What will you do next? What does the team want to do? What are Yani's main social media platforms?

But Estelle's mind kept returning to one simple truth: what had been exposed the night before was just the beginning. The corruption was far more profound than any of them had imagined, and the battle for justice was far from over. She'd already decided she wouldn't back down, no matter how many influential figures stood against her.

At Fael's apartment, the air was filled with a sense of cautious resolve. Fael stared at his phone screen in disbelief as the messages continued to pour in. His hands gripped the device tightly, but he made no move to answer. He felt the shift in the city, the fear in the air, and the undeniable momentum of what they had started. He knew the next steps would require strategy and, above all, control.

Across the street, Christina's apartment felt almost like a bunker, a quiet space for her to work without distractions. She hadn't turned on the television yet, preferring to watch the unfolding chaos from her window. She could see the stirrings of activity on the streets below, small groups gathering, likely discussing the scandal and the government's growing instability.

Christina too had been up all night fielding calls from activists and reporters. She had no idea what would happen next, but one thing was clear: Yani's story had touched something deep within the country's people. Now it was their turn to decide how to proceed.

The morning after the courthouse scandal unfolded, Ari's apartment was tranquil. The chaos and noise of the previous day, the swarming journalists, the heated exchanges, the whispers of corruption that echoed through the streets, seemed to have left a lingering tension in the air. Today, the city was still in shock. But inside his apartment, Ari found a sense of eerie calmness, with the silence only broken by the distant hum of the city below.

The apartment, still meticulously ordered, reflected a moment of stillness after the storm. The soft gray walls and minimalist decor felt oddly comforting, though everything seemed to carry the weight of what had transpired. Ari sat in his favorite armchair by the window, watching the light from the morning sun filter through the blinds, casting long shadows across the wooden floor.

The events of the previous day weighed heavily on his mind. The courthouse erupted into chaos. Yani's trial became an uncontainable spectacle. The fight for justice had escalated beyond the courtroom. The media had made it a circus, and now, as if the world had suddenly shifted, Ari was no longer just a doctor. He was a silent witness to a movement, a moment that might change everything for Yani and for the country.

Yani's face was all over the news. She had stood firm, her every word and action scrutinized, but beneath that strength, Ari knew she was carrying the weight of something much heavier. He had never seen her like this before, not even in the most stressful moments of her work as a detective. But this was different. This wasn't just about cracking a case. This was about exposing a deep-rooted corruption in the heart of the justice system, and she was right at the center of it all.

Ari's phone buzzed on the table beside him, breaking his reverie. It was a text from Estelle, asking if he could take care of and protect Yani. He typed a quick reply, explaining that Yani had retreated into her apartment to avoid the media frenzy. He wanted to give her space to process everything. They both needed time.

Still, a gnawing feeling lingered in his chest. As a doctor, he was trained to treat physical wounds and heal the body. But this was different. His thoughts kept returning to Yani, how her mind must be in turmoil and how her heart must be heavy.

She had trusted and confided in him, but now he felt helpless, caught between his professional duties and his desire to protect her. He missed her laughter, remembering how lighthearted she used to be when they were together before everything took a darker turn. She had always been someone who looked for solutions and leaned on him, but now she was facing a challenge unlike anything she had encountered before. Meanwhile, he felt stuck in this apartment, overwhelmed and feeling useless.

Ari stood up, walked to the window, and looked out onto the bustling street below. It was a new day, but it felt like the city hadn't quite recovered from what had happened in the courthouse. People moved with an air of uncertainty, talking in hushed voices. There was an energy in the air, a charged atmosphere that hinted at something bigger, a revolution, a reckoning.

He returned to the apartment, glancing at the photo of Yani on the coffee table. It was a rare moment of peace amid all the chaos from yesterday. She looked radiant and carefree, as if the world hadn't yet burdened her with its heavy secrets. Ari's fingers traced the edge of the frame, and a small sigh escaped his lips.

Today, he had to find a way to help her. He couldn't just sit back and wait for things to unfold any longer. He needed to be there for her, to stand by her side, even if it meant stepping into a battle far beyond his comfort zone. But first, he needed to see her to ensure she was okay. The world around them was changing, and Ari had a feeling that the next few days would determine the course of everything.

The phone buzzed again, and Ari picked it up. This time, it was a news alert.

Breaking News: The president's office denies involvement in the scandal, but leaked documents confirm presidential awareness of corruption within the judiciary. Ministers and judges reportedly linked to scandal. Public protests expected to escalate.

The words hit him hard. The leaked documents, his mind flashed back to those whispers of state secrets, of the ties between the judiciary and the highest echelons of power. Everything was falling apart, but it wasn't just Yani's case anymore. This was a reckoning for the entire system.

He put the phone down and grabbed his jacket, his resolve hardening. Yani might have been the face of the scandal, but the fight was much bigger than just her. The corruption that had stained the system had been exposed, and now it was time for everyone to answer. And Ari wasn't about to let her face it alone.

The cool morning air greeted him out of the apartment as he walked out.

A sense of dread hung as the morning light filtered through the city's streets. The headlines on every major news outlet painted a grim portrait of a nation on the brink of collapse. The Ogooue

Gazette blared in bold letters across its front page: "MASS SUICIDES SHAKE GOVERNMENT: MINISTERS AND JUDGES DEAD, PUBLIC IN UPROAR."

Just a few blocks away, the Pog Tribune had its damning headline: "SUICIDES OF TOP MINISTERS AND JUDGES SPARK NATIONAL OUTRAGE: GOVERNMENT COLLAPSING UNDER THE WEIGHT OF CORRUPTION." Both newspapers displayed stark images of the faces of the deceased, their deaths a chilling aftermath to the explosive revelations that had flooded the country just hours before.

As copies of the newspapers were distributed, the full weight of the tragedy began to settle in. The justice minister, the defense minister, and several high-ranking judges had been found lifeless in their homes, apparent suicides, a shocking and incongruous end for such influential figures.

News of their deaths spread quickly, the pain of the loss overshadowed only by the growing suspicions of a cover-up. Their involvement in the corruption scandal had been laid bare in the documents released the previous night, confirming their roles in the systematic abuse of power. Yet the question lingered in the minds of many: Were these suicides genuine, or was this the final move in a dark, orchestrated plot to silence the guilty, to protect those still holding onto power?

The public's reaction was immediate and fierce. Outside newsstands and along bustling street corners, people clustered in groups, their faces etched with disbelief and anger. The whispers of what had happened and who was responsible swirled like a tangible force. The tension was palpable, as though the streets were holding their breath.

The air was thick with the buzz of mounting outrage. The previous day's protests, a flash of defiance, now took on a sharper tone, more urgent. People began to fill the streets again, demanding answers, their voices growing louder with each passing moment. Their anger was focused not only on the deceased ministers and judges but squarely at the very top of the government. Many were now calling for the immediate resignation of the president and the prime minister, holding them accountable for the rampant corruption that had seeped into every level of governance.

It wasn't just a political collapse but a crisis of faith. The institutions supposed to protect and serve the public had become the breeding grounds for manipulation and exploitation. The revelation of these dark secrets and the subsequent deaths had ripped the veil away from a system that many now saw as irreparably broken.

Shouts rose as citizens plastered new signs and posters across walls and lampposts. The slogans were simple but fierce: "RESIGN NOW" and "WE DESERVE JUSTICE." For the first time in years, it felt like the people were no longer passive bystanders but active participants in the fight for accountability.

Conversations in cafés, offices, marketplaces, and crowded malls turned to the same burning question: Was this the end of the government's reign, or just the beginning of something even more dangerous? The thought that influential figures were still in the shadows, manipulating events behind closed doors, made people uneasy. Still, it also pushed them to demand a resolution, an end to the corruption that had run rampant for far too long.

The nation seemed to be breathing, waiting for the next move. Would there be further revelations? Would the president and his allies take the fall, or would they find a way to keep their grip on power? Whatever the outcome, one thing was sure: this was only the beginning of a new chapter in the country's struggle for truth and justice.

The public ministries and the presidency exuded an eerie, hollow atmosphere, as if the very essence of authority had been drained from their walls. The once-grandiose structures, symbols of power and control, now felt like monuments to a lost empire, tall, imposing, but empty. The glass-and-steel facades, which had once reflected the brilliance of the nation's leadership, now seemed to sag under the weight of the recent suicides. The sharp sunlight that poured down on the streets outside had a muted, sickly quality, as though it too had been tainted by the scandal that had erupted like wildfire the day before.

Inside the ministries, the mood was a strange kind of paralysis. Where once there had been a flurry of activity, papers shuffled, phones ringing, discussions held behind closed doors, there was now only the deafening silence of resignation. Office doors locked to protect secrets now stood ajar, their insides dark and disheveled. Staff members moved like shadows through the halls, their footsteps soft, their voices hushed, as if afraid to disturb the ghosts of what had been.

Some offices were empty, others slowly being cleared, papers and files hastily thrown into boxes as the last remnants of the ministers' power were carted away.

The once-pristine hallways now seemed cavernous and cold, the marble floors echoing without authority. The photographs of the nation's leaders that lined the walls, faces once full of pride and promise, had taken on an almost mocking quality, as though staring down at the collapse of their legacies. Staff and aides walked in and out of rooms with blank expressions, eyes glazed over as if they'd been pulled into an irreversible spiral of dread. Conversations were whispered, if they occurred at all, and a palpable unease hung like a suffocating fog.

The presidency, the heart of the nation's governance, was cloaked in a similar atmosphere of dread and foreboding. Once alive with the pulse of decisions that shaped the country's future, the vast building now felt abandoned. The corridors were unnaturally quiet, save for the occasional murmur of staff who appeared to be in a trance, moving from one task to the next with mechanical precision. The grand offices, gleaming oak desks, regal chairs, polished floors, felt grotesque in their opulence, starkly contrasting the quiet, tense air that permeated the building.

The president's office, once the epicenter of national power, now seemed like a tomb. The massive oak desk that had once commanded authority now felt like a forgotten relic, its surface littered with unopened letters, dusty files, and empty coffee cups. The once-glowing chandeliers above seemed dim, their light casting long shadows across the room. The president himself, once a towering figure, had vanished into seclusion, his whereabouts unknown, his presence reduced to a distant memory. His aides whispered among themselves, their faces drawn, eyes darting nervously toward the door as if expecting anyone to burst in and demand an answer.

Outside the windows, the capital city reflected the mood within. Once bustling with the energy of people going about their lives, the streets now felt empty and hollow. Citizens moved cautiously, casting wary glances at the towering government buildings as though they too feared the weight of the corruption that had been uncovered. Newsstands were crowded with newspapers bearing grim headlines, but the usual fervor for politics had been replaced with a tense silence. People spoke in hushed tones, as if the air itself were charged with the anger and disbelief that had overtaken the nation.

In the ministries, whispers of the suicides spread like wildfire, though no one could quite shake the suspicion that these deaths were more than they seemed. The suddenness, the horror of it all, left a sour taste in the air. Ministers who had once spoken with authority were now reduced to tragic figures, dead by their own hand or perhaps forced into it, silenced by the truth they had tried to bury. Their private offices, now abandoned, seemed to carry their echoes; the papers left behind, allegations, reports, files detailing the extent of the corruption, served as the final testament to the lives they had built upon lies.

The questions surrounding their deaths remained unanswered, leaving a pervasive sense of unease that refused to dissipate. Was it guilt? Fear of exposure? Or was there something more sinister at play, an orchestrated attempt to avoid the inevitable reckoning that would soon come for everyone involved? Once proud of their power, the ministers now seemed like ghosts, their presence fading from the buildings they had once ruled. Some of the staff, perhaps out of fear or a sense of betrayal, now found themselves trapped between the weight of guilt and a compulsion to carry on, trying to salvage whatever was left of the state's credibility.

The crisp air of early morning felt different, charged with a new sense of urgency. The streets, once bustling with citizens, were now crowded with them, their faces etched with anger, confusion, and determination. People gathered in small clusters around newsstands, their eyes scanning the latest headlines, which deepened their sense of betrayal.

It was still early, but the mood was already electric, like the calm before a storm. The morning sun barely touched the city, as if the day held its breath, waiting for something to break. The protests that had begun the day before were no longer isolated acts of defiance; they had become a groundswell of frustration.

The election had been set for the following year, but now that plan seemed like an eternity away. News broadcasts, once carefully controlled by the government, were now airing damning reports, exposing the corruption that had plagued every corner of the regime. Journalists who had been silenced for years were finally speaking out, their voices a rallying cry for those who had been muted for too long. And the message was clear: the people were done waiting.

The TV channels, now operating with a new sense of boldness, **broadcast** a continual loop of images showing the faces of the ministers, judges, and officials caught in the corruption scandal. In contrast to the usual polished rhetoric of the state-run broadcasts, these programs were filled with footage of outraged citizens in the streets, holding signs demanding accountability, resignation, and an immediate election. The voices of the oppressed were now amplified, reverberating through every corner of the city, challenging the authority that had once kept them in check.

The headlines in the major newspapers were blunt: "GOVERNMENT'S CORRUPTION UNVEILED: RESIGN NOW!" and "PUBLIC CALLS FOR EARLY ELECTION: PRESIDENT'S TIME IS UP." The gravity of the situation was unmistakable. The president, who had once enjoyed the full backing of the state apparatus, now stood on the precipice of history, facing a nation that had turned against him.

In the city's heart, crowds had gathered outside government buildings, chanting in unison, their voices rising in anger. "Resign now! Resign now!" they cried, their fists raised high. The protests were not just an outpouring of outrage over the corruption revealed the day before; they were a collective demand for change, for a new kind of leadership. The people had tasted the bitter fruits of betrayal and were no longer willing to accept the lies and manipulation fed to them for so long.

Even the television channels, which had long been under the government's thumb, began to shift. The familiar faces of anchors who once parroted government rhetoric now sat with a rare, almost defiant expression. Their voices were no longer steady and controlled; their reporting carried an undercurrent of disbelief.

"An unprecedented wave of protests is sweeping the country," one anchor said, her voice steady but tinged with disbelief. "Citizens are demanding that the president and his entire government step down immediately following the release of shocking revelations about widespread corruption at the highest levels of government. The people are calling for an early election, now!"

The news station cut to footage of protesters marching in the streets, their chants growing louder with each passing second. Some carried homemade signs, "DOWN WITH CORRUPTION!" "WE DEMAND JUSTICE!" while others held up photographs of the ministers and judges implicated in the scandal. The scenes were raw, unfiltered, and filled with urgency.

Outside the television station, crowds had gathered, pressing against the gates, calling for the entire government's resignation. Some protesters pounded on the walls of the building, while others stood in silent defiance, their eyes fixed on the television screens through the windows. They had come to demand the truth and witness it being broadcast in real time.

"Turn your backs on them!" shouted one protester, his face painted with the defiance of someone who had been silenced too long. "Let them see that we are done with them! We want an election! An election now!"

As the news continued, more faces appeared on the screens, citizens, activists, and former regime allies who had come forward with their own stories of the corruption they had witnessed. They had all become part of a new movement, one that was no longer content to stay in the shadows, afraid of the powers that had once held them in line.

Inside the government buildings, a sense of unease permeated the air. Ministers huddled in their offices, desperately trying to come up with a response. Some frantically reached out to the president, but there was no reply. Others spoke in hushed tones, wondering if their time was ending.

The minister of foreign affairs sat in his official vehicle, a sleek black sedan crawling along the congested main road. The city buzzed with the tension of a thousand unsaid words, and outside the tinted windows, the world seemed to be closing in. The street was unusually crowded this morning, but it wasn't just the traffic that slowed the minister's journey; it was the seething mass of citizens lining the sidewalks, their eyes burning with resentment.

A woman, sitting behind the wheel of a battered truck, lowered her window. The engine hummed as she leaned out, her face set in a scowl. Her voice rang through the air like a whipcrack.

"Look at this idiot minister wasting our money while we suffer!" she shouted, her words cutting through the city's noise.

A man walking his children to school paused on the sidewalk. His face contorted with anger, and he turned to the car and yelled, "Thieves! Thieves of public funds!" His children tugged at his sleeves, but he didn't flinch. His voice was steady, carrying the weight of a collective frustration building for months.

Around them, the crowd began to swell, murmurs rising into a cacophony of condemnation. The minister, trying to keep his composure, could feel the heat of their stares, like invisible hands pressing down on him. For once, it wasn't the foreign dignitaries, wealthy business people, or powerful elites who controlled the streets; it was the people who were no longer afraid to make their anger known.

As the vehicle inched forward, the minister felt the familiar tension in his chest. The air around him was thick and heavy with the moment's weight. This wasn't just a traffic jam; it was a sign, a sign that the power he'd taken for granted was slipping away, piece by piece, with every insult hurled from the sidewalks.

And still, the car moved forward, just a bit faster now, the city's noise closing in on him like a trap.

Traffic crept forward, but the tension in the air only thickened as the minister's car slowly maneuvered through the throng of angry citizens. Their shouts grew louder and more insistent, as if the ground beneath the vehicle began to tremble with the weight of their collective rage. The sound echoed in the minister's ears, an unrelenting drumbeat of discontent that gnawed at his confidence.

A man standing by the curb, clutching a crumpled newspaper in one hand, stepped into the street, blocking the vehicle's path. With a mocking smile, he raised his free hand and pointed directly at the minister's tinted windows. "Do you know what the people are saying about you?" he yelled, his voice cutting through the chaos. "You've stolen from us, and now you hide behind your walls of glass!"

Inside the vehicle, the minister's grip tightened on the armrest. His thoughts raced, but his mouth remained shut. He couldn't afford to acknowledge them, not when his every move was being watched and scrutinized. But even as his eyes focused on the road ahead, he knew things had changed. The streets no longer felt like a place of order but a battleground where the ordinary citizen had claimed their voice, and it was an angry, unforgiving one.

Then a car honked behind him, the driver growing impatient with the stall. The minister's driver glanced nervously at him through the rearview mirror, but the minister motioned for him to stay calm. The last thing they needed was to escalate the situation further.

Suddenly, a group of young people appeared, faces smeared with defiance and resolve. They marched forward in a loose formation, some holding signs, others chanting slogans, their voices a rising chorus of indignation.

"We want justice!" one of them shouted, raising their fist. "Down with the thieves!" The crowd that had been merely vocal before began to shift, rallying behind these new voices. The movement was no longer passive; it was gathering force.

The minister's pulse quickened. The protesters weren't just angry; they were organized. He could feel the unmistakable shift from a spontaneous outburst of frustration to something more focused, more dangerous. A surge of panic began to bubble inside him. He couldn't remember the last time he had felt this vulnerable.

His eyes darted to the rearview mirror again as the sound of clanging pots and pans, an unmistakable sign of protest, echoed behind him. It was like a storm gathering on the horizon, and now it was crashing down in waves, each more forceful than the last.

As the protesters drew closer to the car, the minister's driver put the vehicle in gear and tried to edge forward, but the path was blocked. The crowd wasn't moving, their voices drowning out the engine's sound.

A young woman holding an "ENOUGH IS ENOUGH" sign stepped forward and tapped the window. She looked directly at the minister, her eyes steady and unyielding.

"This is the last time you hide behind your office," she said coldly. "The people see you for what you are."

The minister's breath caught in his throat, and for the first time in years, he felt the crushing weight of his powerlessness. His mind raced, trying to think of a way out, but all that seemed to surround him now were angry faces and the knowledge that his world was crumbling around him.

Seeing the situation spiraling out of control, the driver revved the engine in a last-ditch effort to push through, but the crowd was relentless. The protests were no longer a distant echo; they were at his doorstep, in his face, demanding answers.

And so the minister of foreign affairs sat in his official vehicle, surrounded by the weight of the city's rage, his future uncertain. All that was left was the suffocating sense that the power he had so carefully clung to was slipping away, one protest, one shout, one challenge at a time.

The tension in the air thickened as the insults continued to echo through the street. The minister of foreign affairs sat rigid in the back of his official vehicle, his eyes darting between the faces pressed against the tinted windows. He had hoped for a quick escape, a smooth ride back to his office. Instead, he was trapped in a sea of enraged citizens, their fury pouring over him like a deluge.

Young men gathered near the intersection, their chants growing louder. "Thieves! Liars! Out with the corrupt!" One of them shook his fist at the car, the veins in his neck pulsing with anger.

The minister's driver, a seasoned man who had seen his share of protests, stared out the front windshield with frustration and helplessness.

"We're stuck, sir," he muttered, glancing nervously in the rearview mirror at the growing crowd. "They won't let us through."

The minister's mind raced. This was no longer just a matter of political embarrassment; it was dangerous. The crowd could turn violent if they remained in this spot for too long. His heart pounded as he considered the worst-case scenario, but then came a flash of clarity. He could still salvage this, but only if he acted quickly.

Taking a deep breath, he reached for his phone, dialed his aide, and spoke in a hushed, urgent voice. "I need a plan. Get me a way out of here...now."

Within seconds, the minister's phone buzzed again. His aide had worked quickly, tapping into his connections and calling in favors. A diversion was coming, a small window of opportunity to break through the crowd and avoid further escalation.

"Sir," the driver said, looking over at him. "There's a way out through the side streets, but it's tight. We'll need to move fast."

The minister nodded, steadying his nerves. "Do it. Take us around the back."

With a careful maneuver, the driver eased the car into the narrower lane, steering away from the protesters who continued to shout their condemnation. The crowd, now more concentrated in front of the car, didn't notice the vehicle slipping away to the side. It wasn't a flawless escape, but it was enough.

Just as they descended into a quieter road, the minister's phone buzzed again. A notification appeared on his screen, a live broadcast from a central news station. The shot was taken from an aerial view, showing the protesters and the vehicle's escape route. A headline flashed at the bottom of the screen: "MINISTER OF FOREIGN

AFFAIRS NARROWLY ESCAPES PUBLIC OUTRAGE IN A TENSE SITUATION."

His heart sank, knowing the image would be all over the news. Yet it wasn't the worst outcome. It was a controlled escape; he wasn't wholly humiliated in the public's eye. He could still work the narrative and spin the situation in his favor.

"Keep going," he said, leaning back in his seat, trying to calm his racing thoughts. "We need to go straight to the office. I have a plan, but we must meet with the others as soon as possible."

The car drove on, the noise of the protest fading in the distance. Despite the tension, the minister's mind was already shifting into problem-solving mode. His immediate survival was secured, but the real challenge was ahead: he needed to find a way to make the public believe he was doing everything to clean up the corruption and restore their trust. He'd have to move fast. There wasn't much time left.

Minutes later, the car rolled into the ministry of foreign affairs' private parking garage. The minister stepped out, straightened his suit, and walked briskly into the building.

As he entered the meeting room, his aides and senior staff were waiting. The tension was palpable, but everyone knew what needed to be done.

"We have to make a public statement immediately," he said, his voice firm. "We tell them we're starting a full investigation into all claims of corruption and abuse of power. We distance ourselves from yesterday's events and promise swift action…no stone left unturned."

One of his aides looked at him nervously. "And if the people don't buy it, sir?"

He paused, looking at the faces of those who had always followed his lead. He knew they expected him to pull off the impossible.

"Then," he said, a slight smirk crossing his lips, "we give them what they want: an early election. But only under the right circumstances. It's time to use our position to turn the tide in our favor."

The room murmured approval. His plan was risky, but it was a way out. If he could manage the fallout from the protests and the media coverage, it would placate the public, give them the illusion of power, and buy him time to clean the house.

As the minutes ticked by, the minister felt the weight of the crisis beginning to lift. Though embarrassing, his escape from the crowd had allowed him to regain control. The following steps would be crucial, but the immediate danger had passed.

The minister stepped away from the table, his fingers trembling slightly as he dialed the president's number. The screen flashed with the president's name, and he took a deep breath before answering. The air around him seemed to thicken with every passing second.

"Mr. President," the minister said as the line clicked, his voice steady but tight with urgency. "I've briefed the team. We're moving forward with a statement, but we need to get ahead of this before it turns into a wildfire. The public's demands are escalating—"

"Don't tell me about the damn public," the president's voice cut through sharply. "I've heard enough of that. It's not just the people. It's the whole damn country that's about to collapse."

The minister froze for a moment, his stomach sinking. He could hear the anger in the president's voice, but more than that, there was fear. A fear he hadn't expected. "Sir, what do you mean? We've handled crises before. We can stabilize this."

"No, you don't understand. This is different," the president said, his tone lowering. "I'm done with the lies. The corruption has gone too deep. It's not just a few bad apples anymore. It's the whole damn orchard. If we keep lying to the people, it will not just be a protest. It will become something worse. It could trigger a civil war."

The minister's mind raced, processing the gravity of the situation. Civil war? That wasn't what he'd anticipated, and he certainly couldn't handle it. "Sir, what are you suggesting?"

A heavy silence followed, and then the president sighed deeply, a weariness in his voice that the minister rarely heard. "I don't know how long I can keep this charade up. The country is on the brink, and we both know it. If I continue with this…corruption investigation and the talk of cleanups, people will see right through it. They'll know it's a lie. We're at the edge of a precipice, and I'm not sure I can stop the fall."

The minister felt the weight of the words. It was one thing to manage a scandal and another entirely to face the nation's breakdown. He had been calculating risks and preparing for the fallout, but this? This was something else.

"We can still turn this around, sir. We can manage the narrative, buy time, and show the world we're taking action. But we'll need a public face…a new direction. A real investigation. You can't keep this up, not now."

The president was quiet momentarily, then spoke again, his voice raw. "And what do you suggest? Your colleague's spokesperson committed suicide this morning. I need you. Do you want me to step down? Announce my resignation?"

"No, no," the minister replied quickly. "Not yet, Mr. President. But we have to look like we're responding. It's the only way out. We give them something they can hold on to…a promise of new elections. People love democracy. They believe in it. We'll turn the narrative on its head. It's the only way they'll give us another chance."

There was a long pause. Finally, the president spoke again, his voice softer but resolute. "Fine. Please do it. Announce a new election. But you must clarify that this is the only way we'll rebuild the trust. If the people want to vote me out, so be it. But they have to know I am doing this for them. I'll take the high road, and they'll see it. They'll give me a second chance, and when they do, I'll finish what I started."

The minister felt a chill run down his spine. He could hear the finality in the president's tone, the faint hope that the public, in their naivety, would see through the rhetoric. But he also knew the risks involved, if the people rejected the president now, it could all collapse. And if they bought the facade, it would only prolong the inevitable.

"Understood, Mr. President. I'll have a statement ready." He looked back at his aides, giving them a quick, almost imperceptible nod.

"Good. And make sure it's convincing," the president said before the line went dead with a sharp click.

The minister lowered the phone and looked up at his team. "He knew the risks involved. If the people rejected the president now, it could all collapse. And if they bought the facade, it would only prolong the inevitable."

One of his aides hesitated, then asked, "But what if they don't buy it, sir? What if they see it for what it is?"

The minister swallowed, his doubt gnawing at him, but he couldn't afford to show it. "Then we'll handle it. We'll spin it. We'll do what we have to.

Right now, the only thing we can control is the message. We need to make them believe this is for them."

As the team moved into action, the minister's phone buzzed again. This time, it was his spokesperson. He quickly pressed the call button.

"Sir, we've prepared a draft for the statement," the spokesperson said, a sense of urgency in their voice. "We can go live in fifteen minutes. You ready for this?"

The minister paused, looking at the gathered faces around him. His mind raced; he could see the path forward, but at what cost? If the public saw through this ruse.

The room buzzed with activity as the minister's aides scrambled to fine-tune the details. The statement needed to be flawless. A calculated blend of sincerity and political acumen, the kind that could sell the notion of a new election as a move toward the country's restoration.

Minutes passed like hours. The minister's mind was elsewhere, focusing on the next step, on the fallout that was bound to come. What would the opposition say? What would the media spin? The whispers of civil unrest were growing louder, and it seemed that even the president's desperate attempt to regain the people's favor might not be enough to stop the tide of discontent.

"Sir, the draft is ready," one of the aides said, breaking his thoughts. "Would you like to review it before we go live?"

The minister glanced at the paper in the aide's hands, then back at his team. "No time for reviews. Just make sure it sounds real."

The aide nodded and went to the podium, adjusting the microphone. The minister moved toward the corner of the room, phone in hand, staring out the window at the distant skyline, where the distant sounds of protests still carried an ever-present reminder of the storm threatening to break.

As he walked to the podium, the camera zoomed in on the minister, his face a mask of controlled urgency. Behind him, a large screen displayed a carefully prepared slogan about national renewal, the kind of political theater meant to calm a restless public. The room was silent as he adjusted the microphone, his demeanor calm despite the storm brewing outside.

"Good evening," the minister began, his voice echoing in the silent room. "I stand before you today, not just as a servant of this government, but as a representative of the people of this nation. The past few days have made it clear that our country is at a crossroads. The calls for justice, accountability, and change cannot be ignored."

He paused, allowing the weight of his words to settle in the room. The media were hanging on every syllable, cameras clicking, reporters scribbling.

"We have heard your voices," he continued. "The people of this nation are not just protesting. They are demanding transparency, justice, and a government that truly serves them. And let me be clear, we will deliver. Despite our challenges, the president of this Republic is committed to seeing this through. We are not afraid of the truth. We will confront it head-on."

There was a brief flicker of doubt in his mind, but the minister pushed it down. He needed the illusion of control, the facade of a government willing to listen.

"As part of our commitment to reform, I am announcing today that the president will call for an early election. This is not just a promise. It is an act of faith in our people and the democratic process. The election will be free, fair, and transparent... an opportunity for the citizens of this country to choose their future, to take control of the direction of our great nation."

The minister's voice grew stronger, his confidence bolstered by the rehearsed lines. "We understand the anger, the frustration, the fear. These are difficult times, but we believe that through the power of democracy, we can emerge from this crisis stronger than ever. This will be our chance to rebuild, heal, and move forward together."

He paused again, letting the weight of the statement sink in.

"I call on all parties, all citizens, to unite in this endeavor. It is time to move beyond division and focus on what truly matters, the future of this country. The president and I are committed to ensuring that this process is conducted with integrity and fairness, and we will hold those accountable who have betrayed the people's trust. Our mission is clear, restore justice, restore hope, and restore the future of our children."

The minister gave a brief nod, signaling the end of the statement. The cameras flashed as the room erupted in questions, but he was already stepping away from the podium, his eyes focused on the screen before him. He had played his part. Now, it was up to the president, up to the people.

The room in the minister's inner offices had gone deathly quiet. The minister sat at his desk, tapping the surface almost unconsciously. His phone buzzed again. It was the president.

He answered quickly. "Mr. President."

The president's voice was strained, thin with exhaustion, but there was a sense of cautious optimism there. "It's done. The announcement... it's out there. The ball's in their court now."

The minister leaned back in his chair, rubbing his temples. "We'll see if they buy it. It's a risk, sir. The people are angry, and they're looking for blood."

"I know," the president said, his voice lowering. "But we have to try at least. If they reject it, I'll step down. If they accept it, we get another chance. But we can't just sit back and wait for them to tear us apart."

The minister's fingers tightened around the edge of his desk, his nails pressing into the wood. "We can only hope they don't see through the act, sir. If they don't, we could be looking at another revolution."

There was a long silence on the other end of the line. Finally, the president spoke firmly, his voice a mixture of hope and resignation. "Then we prepare for the worst. And pray that the worst doesn't come."

The minister hung up, his stomach a knot of unease. He glanced out the window again. The protests hadn't stopped. The people were still there, waiting. The next few days, maybe even hours, would determine whether this was the start of a new chapter, or the beginning of something far darker.

As he left the room, his aides followed closely behind, a cloud of doubt hanging over them. The minister's mind raced with thoughts. There were still so many variables and uncertainties. The announcement was only the beginning; the real battle was yet to come. Would the election quell the unrest, or would the people rise up even more? One thing was certain: the game had begun, and it was a dangerous one.

CHAPTER 10

The morning unfolds gently, a soft symphony of light and sound. The first rays of the sun stretch slowly across the horizon, spilling warmth over the land. The sky, a delicate blend of pink and gold, glows with a quiet promise as the day begins. A cool breeze whispers through the air, moving with a purpose, brushing the wildflowers that dot the meadow like scattered jewels. Their petals tremble and sway, caught in the dance of the wind. The flowers, bright yellows, purples, and deep reds, seem to stretch toward the light, their colors vivid against the pale morning.

A handful of birds have perched on the flowers, some on the delicate stems, others fluttering through the air, their feathers catching the soft light. The birds sing, high, lilting notes that echo through the calm air, their melodies blending with the rustling of leaves and the distant hum of nature waking up. The world feels alive in the quietest, most peaceful way.

The scent of fresh earth and blooming petals drifts through the breeze, filling the air with a natural sweetness. Every breath feels full and rich, the air crisp and clean. The sun's warmth begins to chase away the coolness of the morning, touching everything with its gentle fingers and coaxing the world into motion.

There is a sense of peace in the stillness and a subtle pull, a quiet invitation. As the light grows, it beckons you forward to take a step, feel the warmth on your skin, and walk into the day ahead. The town lies just beyond the horizon, its outlines soft but clear, waiting with its energy, its rhythm.

With a soft exhale, you begin to walk. The earth beneath your feet is cool, but the air around you is warm, and the breeze continues to stir the flowers, their soft motion in rhythm with your own. The birds continue to sing, their songs following you like a soft background melody as you make your way toward the town, your steps light, the world around you unfolding in perfect harmony.

The room was tense, the air thick with purpose. Yani and her lawyers sat around a large conference table in a small, dimly lit office. A monitor on the wall displayed the latest news broadcast of the minister's press statement. His carefully constructed words echoed in their minds, each a strategic move to placate the angry masses and sell the idea of a "new" election that would hopefully give the president a fresh shot at power.

Estelle leaned forward, her eyes sharp, analyzing every word. "They think the people are stupid," she said, calm but contemptuous. "This whole election idea? It's just a diversion. A way to put a bandage over a gaping wound. They're betting that the anger will dissipate once they give the illusion of democracy."

Ari, who had been listening quietly, crossed his arms. "Could we counter with a statement of our own? Just throw out our narrative to expose the government for the frauds they are?"

David shook his head slowly, his expression thoughtful. "A statement is easy, but it's just words. Words won't move the people. We can't just call them liars and walk away. We need to act. What we say has to be backed up by what we do."

Fael and Christina, quiet up to this point, exchanged looks. Christina spoke first, her voice steady but uncertain.

"What else can we do? We have to get the people on our side. But how do we break their trust in the government? How do we expose the truth in a way that forces the system to respond?" Fael asked.

Carlos, pacing near the window, turned to face the group. "We give the people hope. Real hope. The government's election isn't about restoring power to the people. It's about maintaining the status quo. We must show them a different path, something they can believe in. They need to know there's a way out of this."

Yani, who had been silent, taking everything in, stood up suddenly. Her voice cut through the room with a quiet but undeniable strength. "I'll make the statement. Not through the lawyers, not through another face or spokesperson. I will make the statement."

The room fell into silence as everyone turned toward her. Yani's gaze was unwavering, her resolve clear. She knew exactly what she was proposing, and it was a game changer.

"You want to confront the government head-on?" Ari asked, his voice tinged with surprise. "They'll try to discredit you. They'll call you a threat, an enemy of the state."

Yani's eyes locked onto his. "Let them. I'll show them that I'm not afraid of their lies. I'll expose everything: the corruption, the manipulation, the deception. And then I'll declare my candidacy for the early election they're pushing. Not to play their game but to change it. To give the people something real to fight for."

The others exchanged glances. Ari nodded slowly. "I like it. But you're putting yourself on the line. This is more than just politics now. They'll come after you."

Yani smiled faintly. "Let them. This isn't just about me. It's about all of us. The people are angry. They're scared. And they're looking for someone to lead them. I'm done hiding in the shadows. If I have to put my badge on the line to show them the truth, then so be it."

David's expression softened with approval. "I agree. It's bold, it's risky, but it could work. You can't just fight the system with words. You have to give the people something to rally behind. You have to be the alternative. And they'll listen to you."

Carlos spoke up next, his tone thoughtful. "It'll be hard, though. The government will attack you with everything they have. They'll use the media to paint you as dangerous, as a threat to national security. You have to be ready for that."

"I'm ready," Yani replied, her voice steady. "It's the only way we can beat them. I'll announce my resignation from the police force, and in the same breath, I'll declare my candidacy. It's risky, but we don't have the luxury of caution anymore. We won't just challenge their lies. We'll show the people that there's someone who truly understands what they're going through, someone who's been in the fight all along."

Estelle gave a small smile, clearly impressed. "You're going to have to be relentless. We all will. We can't back down. If we do, they win. But if we stand firm, if we show the people that we're serious,"

"They'll stand with us," Yani finished. "Exactly."

The team fell into a brief but significant silence, considering the weight of Yani's proposal. Then one by one, they nodded. It was unbelievably risky, but it was the only way to pierce the veil the government had erected around itself.

Ari grinned, a fire in his eyes. "I'm in. Let's bring the truth down on them, all of it."

David stood too, his voice confident. "We'll need to get ahead of the narrative. I'll start to write Yani's resignation, gather evidence, and document everything. We'll make sure they can't turn this back on us."

Fael's eyes glinted with determination. "And we'll get the people's backing. We'll organize rallies and spread the word."

The days that followed were a blur of planning, strategy, and nonstop action. Yani and her team wasted no time executing her bold plan. Her decision to resign from the police force and her intention to run for the upcoming election spread like wildfire, igniting hope and sparking fierce debate. The government's media machine scrambled to contain the damage, but the truth was already out there. Yani had made her move.

The press conference was in a small but intimate venue, carefully chosen for its symbolism. It was in a gritty city, where the protests had been the loudest, and promises had never been fulfilled by the government. The place was brimming with reporters, cameras, and anticipation.

Yani walked into the room, her posture straight and confident, the weight of the moment pressing down on her shoulders. This wasn't just a statement;

it was a declaration of war against the system that had betrayed the people for far too long.

She stepped up to the podium, her eyes scanning the room. Every face in the crowd was eager for her words, hungry for something real in a time of lies. The cameras clicked incessantly, but she remained calm and composed. She wasn't just a former police officer now; she was a rallying point, the one person in the country who wasn't afraid to speak the truth.

The room quieted as she began.

"Good afternoon. I stand before you today, not as an official of the state or a servant of a corrupt government, but as a citizen of this country. And like so many of you, I am tired. Tired of the lies. Tired of the manipulation. Tired of being treated like we don't matter."

Her words struck deep, and she could see the reporters leaning in, hanging on every syllable.

"I have spent years working as a police officer, trying to protect the people and do my job despite the system working against us. But I can no longer be part of a machine that upholds corruption, shields those in power from accountability, and allows the people to suffer while the elites grow wealthier and more entrenched in their corruption."

Yani paused, her gaze sweeping across the room, locking eyes with several key reporters. She wasn't just speaking to them but to the nation.

"Today, I resign from my position as a police officer. Not because I no longer believe in the duty to protect, but because I can no longer protect a system that needs to be dismantled. And with that, I announce my candidacy for the upcoming election. I will fight for a new beginning. A new future. A future where the people no longer beg for scraps from the table of the rich but demand to sit at the table and decide their fate."

There was a brief, stunned silence in the room. The reporters exchanged glances, some surprised, others already preparing their follow-up questions.

"I know that many of you may doubt me. The government is already spreading lies about me. They will say that I am a threat, that I am dangerous. They will say that I'm doing this for personal gain. But you all know the truth. The truth is that I am doing this because I believe in the people of this country. I believe that we can build something better. And I believe we can do it together."

The tension in the room was palpable. Yani's words were sharp and biting but hopeful. She wasn't just challenging the government but offering a different path based on trust, unity, and action.

"I've heard the cries of the people," she continued. "I've seen the anger, the frustration, the hope in your eyes. You are not alone in this fight.

Together, we can take our future back. Together, we can reclaim our democracy."

Her final words hit like a hammer.

"But I am not just running for office. I am running to give you a voice. I am running to destroy the system that has failed you. If the government truly believes in democracy, then it should have no fear of free elections. They should have no fear of the people choosing their destiny. We will see their true face if they are afraid and try to block this election. And I, for one, will not back down."

The news spread like wildfire. Social media exploded with support and criticism, but one thing was sure: Yani had captured the public's attention. Her words had struck a nerve with the people, and the government was on the defensive for the first time in a long while.

In the days that followed, Yani's team went into overdrive. Estelle coordinated with grassroots activists, urging people to organize rallies and protests to support Yani's candidacy. David and Ari worked tirelessly to gather evidence of the government's corruption, from financial mismanagement to human rights abuses. The aim was precise: to challenge the government's narrative and expose the ugly truth beneath the surface.

Meanwhile, Carlos worked on a media strategy. He aimed to ensure that Yani's message of hope and change reached every corner of the country.

"We need to show the people that this election isn't just a formality," he said one evening, his voice urgent. "It's a battle for the soul of the country. We must make them believe we're not just another voice in the crowd. We're the voice that will lead them out of this nightmare."

As rallies began to spring up across the nation, Yani's message spread beyond just the capital city. From the slums to the middle-class neighborhoods, people were starting to listen. There was a palpable sense of energy in the air, something had shifted, and the government's hold on the people was beginning to loosen.

But the fight was far from over. The government, fearing the loss of power, began to retaliate. They moved to discredit Yani in every way possible, calling her a "traitor," a "puppet of foreign interests," and a "danger to national security." They threatened to use the police force to crack down on rallies, and the military was placed on high alert. But none of this seemed to dampen the rising tide of support for Yani.

The tension in the streets was rising. The people were preparing for the battle of their lives, and in the eye of the storm stood Yani, steadfast, resolute, and determined.

With the election date looming, Yani's team knew they had only a limited time to turn the tide. Every day felt like a countdown to something monumental. As the government prepared to push back with everything it had, Yani stood firm, her resolve more potent than ever.

The people had chosen her; now it was time to deliver. The country's future, perhaps her own, hung in the balance.

Would the government allow the election to proceed? Or would they crack down and risk a full-scale revolution?

Yani knew one thing for sure: the fight had only just begun.

Tensions swelled in the streets, thick like the humidity of a storm about to break. The air hummed with anticipation, but there was no lightning, only the slow, grinding pressure of a society teetering on the edge of collapse. Yani stood in the center of it, motionless as a rock, unbothered by the chaos surrounding her. She had become something other than herself: a symbol, a question hanging in the air that no one could reasonably answer.

The election date loomed, with it, the weight of an unavoidable fate. It wasn't so much the date itself that held any real significance; dates were merely markers in time, irrelevant in the face of an overwhelming absurdity. The expectation made this moment different, as if the world, in its disillusionment, had collectively agreed to bet on the possibility of change. But Yani knew that nothing could change. There was no salvation in politics, only the futile struggle for something that might never come.

People moved around her, their faces a mixture of hope and despair. It was as if they knew the system was broken but couldn't help but hope it might somehow be fixed. Their desire for revolution was a defiance of the absurd, a rejection of a world where the future was never guaranteed, where promises were always empty. And yet they hoped.

Her team buzzed around her, trying to predict the next move. David, her attorney who later became her campaign manager, furrowed his brow with anxiety as he paced back and forth. The moment's urgency consumed him, and his mind raced through strategies that would never alter the outcome.

"The government will clamp down soon," he said, eyes flicking toward the horizon as if the distant future could be seen from here. "They won't let this go any further. We need to act now."

Yani didn't move. She hadn't moved in what felt like days. It wasn't apathy, something more fundamental, something closer to resignation.

"Act how?" she asked quietly, her voice carrying a weight that seemed at odds with the frantic energy of the room.

"They'll suppress us," David insisted, almost pleading. "We need to be ready. We need to show the people we deserve their hope."

Yani's lips parted in a faint smile, but there was no humor. "Ready for what? The inevitable?" Her gaze drifted to the crowd outside, a sea of nameless faces gathered for something that felt, even to them, fragile. "This isn't resistance. It's the illusion of action. It's like holding a match to the ocean and thinking you've set fire to it."

David fell silent, momentarily at a loss. The truth, if one could call it that, sat uncomfortably in the air. Yani wasn't just a candidate; she embodied a question no one dared to ask: "What's the point of fighting if everything we fight for is doomed to fail?"

The streets outside were loud, but their clamor felt muted, like the noise of a passing train that you know will soon disappear into the distance. The people had gathered behind Yani; the same goal united them. They were a collection of individuals, each one searching for meaning in a world that no longer made sense. The idea of change, of victory, had become a desperate hope, a hope that would either be extinguished or outlast the absurdity of it all.

"I'm not asking you to resist," Yani said, finally looking at David. "I'm asking you to accept what's coming. The government will strike. They will use their force. And we will be indestructible, just as the people they have tried to crush before us, they are always going to be losers," she gestured to the street, the people, the world beyond, "and that is the absurdity of it. And it is the absurdity that we must live with, not in defiance, but by conviction."

David stared at her, and for the first time, hope flickered in his eyes. But there wasn't time to talk more. The government had already begun its preparations. It would impose curfews and send soldiers into the streets, their presence both a threat and a mockery of the people's hope. The inevitability of it all loomed over them like an approaching storm.

Meanwhile, in the quiet, airless room of the presidential palace, the government plotted its response. Sitting behind a massive wooden desk, the president looked at the report in his hands with the detached air of someone whose world had long been divorced from any genuine human feeling.

The numbers on the paper meant nothing to him, no more than the faces in the streets. His advisors spoke of tactical maneuvers, the plan to personalize law, and how best to suppress the growing unrest, but their words were hollow. The absurdity of their positions and control was not lost on him. He had spent his entire life holding onto power, but it was clear that no amount of force could hold back the tide forever. His power was as fragile as any other illusion.

"They're already organizing," Elena, his chief of staff, said. "They won't stop. You need to move now, or it could be too late."

The president nodded, his gaze distant.

The president sat alone in his office, the weight of the report in his hands light as a ghost and yet somehow unbearable. The wooden desk was solid, indifferent, still, but his existence here, in this place, seemed to dissolve beneath him. The words on the page, a series of numbers, calculations, and strategies, no longer had the gravity they once had. They were empty, like the world he now lived in. What was the point of having power when it slipped away at the drop of a hat? What was the point of controlling the future when the future was nothing but a cruel mirage?

He put the paper down, his fingers curling around it, feeling its incredible, impersonal texture. And yet it meant nothing. His world was no longer bound up in the simple mechanics of authority; it had become a theater of gestures, an endless loop of posture and pretense. He had spent his life learning the art of manipulation, creating a web of influence, an architecture of control. But now, standing on the precipice of a world teetering toward revolution, even his web was a fragile illusion.

The connection, the impending revolt, and the chaos in the streets seemed too far away. Rebellion was an abstract concept, something distant, outside his reach. His gaze slid off the page, his eyes empty as they rested on the thick velvet curtains that hid the window. Outside, the world was a jumble of agitation. Faces, people's faces, gathered, rose, swelled against him.

He could almost see them, but it was as if they existed only in his mind, a blur of colors and emotions that he could no longer distinguish. They had no identity, no substance to him. He had made them a concept, a mere backdrop for his scene. And now they were breaking free of the script.

"They're already organizing," Elena's voice cut through the thick air, her words slicing through the silence like a blade. She stood beside him, hands clasped behind her back, her tone clear and crisp. "They won't stop. You have to act now, or it could be too late."

Her words echoed, each syllable hanging in the air like an accusation. Too late? What did that mean? Too late for what? Too late to control, to subjugate? It was too late to impose his will on people conditioned to obey. A sense of finality in her tone shook something deep within him. But he didn't move. His body remained rooted to the chair as if rising would require a monumental effort, an act of faith he was no longer capable of.

He nodded slowly, but the gesture was mechanical, meaningless. It was a reflex, an empty act of recognition. He had been nodding for years, nodding to appease others, nodding to move the wheels of power, nodding at his reflection in the mirror, hoping it would somehow fill the void inside him.

"I know," he whispered, the words falling from his mouth as if they were foreign to him. They had no force, no weight. They were as hollow as his understanding of the world.

Elena still stood there, her presence a stark reminder of her role in his theater, an actress reciting the lines of someone who still believed in the charade. But he could see the hollow core beneath her urgency now. She too was a prisoner of absurdity, trapped in the very system they had built together. There was no way forward. She knew it, and yet she persisted. She demanded action.

But what action was left? What could he do?

He turned his eyes to the window, even though he knew he could no longer look at the world the same way. The once so familiar streets outside now seemed like a distant stage where people moved but no longer mattered. They had ceased to be real, just as he had ceased to be essential to them. All that remained was an overwhelming sense of futility, the knowledge that no matter how many soldiers he sent or laws he made, it would all collapse into nothingness.

Yani, the insurgent, the symbol of this revolution, what was she? What was she? She was just a woman standing in the center of a group of people who had had enough of this charade. A mirror that reflected the truth of her existence: that his power had never been real, only the appearance of power. And now, she had torn that illusion apart.

Elena stood silently, watching the president as if seeing him for the first time. He was no longer the figure of unshakable authority she had spent years serving. Instead, he seemed like a man adrift in his world, who had lost sight of what he had once believed to be true. The room felt colder now, as if the walls were closing in. The weight of his words hung between them, not just a moment of doubt but the culmination of a lifetime spent clinging to illusions.

"You can't be serious," she said at last, though there was no conviction in her voice, only the bitter taste of resignation. She had asked him to act, take charge, and do what was necessary to quell the rebellion. But now she understood. He was no longer the president; he was just another man, undone by his contradictions and trapped by his choices.

The president opened his eyes slowly, and for the first time, he truly looked at her. There was no malice in his gaze, no scorn, only the emptiness of a man who had seen through the veil.

"Serious? What does that even mean?" His voice was quiet now, almost reflective. "I have been serious my whole life, Elena. I have lived with that seriousness. But what has it brought me? Nothing.

I've built an empire on the fear of others, a house of cards. And now, now I can see it for what it is. The absurdity is overwhelming."

Elena clenched her fists, fighting the urge to scream. How could he speak so calmly, as if the whole world wasn't about to fall apart? "You're talking like a man who has given up!" she snapped, her voice rising despite herself. "We have everything to lose. The military, the laws, the control. You still have the means to stop this!"

"Stop it?" he repeated, almost amused. "Stop it for what? So I can delay the inevitable? So I can watch it crumble more slowly, piece by piece? I have seen the truth, Elena. I have seen how fragile it all is." He looked down at his hands, fingers curling into the desk's wood. "Control is a game we play to distract ourselves from the void. The people are not fighting for freedom. They are fighting for meaning in a world with none."

Elena took a step back, her expression hardening. She wanted to yell, demand that he take responsibility, pull himself together, and act. She wanted him to be the leader he had always promised to be. But she knew, deep down, that the man in front of her was already beyond that. There was no return from where he had gone, no path back to the power he once wielded.

"Then what do you want me to do?" she asked, her voice strained. "What do you expect from me now? Should I walk away? Let everything burn?"

The president's eyes lifted from the desk, meeting hers. "You ask me what to do, but what is there to do, Elena? We are all just moments in time, fleeting and inconsequential. You, me, Yani, the people in the streets, all of us are fighting against something that cannot be changed. Do you think I have the answers? That I can wield the power to turn this around? I can't even hold onto my sense of self." He shook his head, a thin smile tugging at his lips. "You're asking me to do something, but nothing is left to do. The question is, can we live with it? Can we live with the knowledge that everything we believed in was nothing but a pretense?"

Elena's mouth went dry. She didn't know how to respond. She had spent so many years justifying her loyalty to him, explaining the world they had built, but now, now the world seemed like a flimsy facade. The truth he was speaking felt like a weight in her chest, unbearable yet undeniable.

Outside, she could hear the distant sounds of chanting and the growing murmur of a crowd. The rebellion was moving forward. It was happening, whether the president wanted to face it or not. But it no longer seemed to matter. Nothing seemed to matter.

For a long moment, they stood in silence, the air thick with the tension of unspoken truths. Then, with a sigh, the president stood up from his chair.

He walked over to the window, staring at the city. "I always thought I could control everything. But now I see that all we can control is how we face what is coming. And perhaps, how we face our end."

Elena moved closer to him but couldn't bring herself to touch him. The man before her was no longer the president she had once admired; he was disintegrating, coming apart under the pressure of his existence. She had seen leaders break before and crack under the weight of their choices, but never like this, never with such clarity.

"What are you going to do?" she asked softly, almost afraid of the answer.

The president turned to her then, his face pale, his eyes darker than ever. "What can I do, Elena? The game is over. The pieces are scattered. We are nothing but echoes now. There is no more doing. There is only the waiting."

Elena left the president's office without a word, her heels clicking sharply on the marble floor, a staccato rhythm that echoed through the cold, sterile hallway. She didn't look back. The door swung closed behind her with a hollow finality, the dull thud marking the end of something, something far more significant than the conversation that had just transpired. The door, or even her departure, didn't signify the break. It was the space left in the room. The space between him and the world, the space between the president and what he once thought was his to command.

Outside, the world had already begun to forget him.

In the brief silence that followed her exit, the president remained seated at his desk, hands limp, resting on the smooth surface as if he could draw some last shred of meaning from the cool wood. He looked down at his hands; their absurdity struck him, though he didn't laugh. The realization that his hands, once so accustomed to grasping, to holding power, were now empty and useless was more terrifying than he had anticipated. He had been clutching at this illusion for so long, wrapping himself in the weight of his office, pretending that control was his. But now, in the solitude of the office, he understood that he was not the one in control.

Elena's departure was more than a rupture in their conversation. It was the rupture of an entire world where he had existed as a leader and symbol of authority. Her absence was not personal; it was existential. She had taken with her the last vestiges of his illusion of meaning, the remnants of a system crumbling under the sheer weight of its emptiness. She had abandoned him, not because of some moral failing, but because of a truth they both knew but dared not speak: nothing was left to hold onto.

He stared out the window, but his eyes did not see the streets below. They saw only the reflection of the man in the glass, a man whose face was no longer recognizable. The reflection was an image he had constructed over the years, a projection of power, certainty, and control. But now it seemed foreign. Now it was a shadow, a mere ghost of a man with no substance. He was no longer the president; he was nothing, and the nothingness settled on him with the weight of a thousand unspoken truths.

The clock ticked steadily in the corner of the room, marking time as it always had. But time itself no longer mattered. It had become irrelevant. Each tick was a reminder of his irrelevance. His power, which he had once believed to be an extension of himself, was merely an accident of history, an absurd accident that would soon be corrected. The people outside, the soldiers who had once saluted him with such deference, the advisers who had clung to his every word, all of them had begun to see through the thin veneer of authority. And now they had moved on. The streets had become their stage. The revolution was already unfolding.

His body stiffened, though he made no move to stand. The tension in his chest was not physical; it was existential. He had spent his entire life fabricating a self, a narrative of power, righteousness, and inevitability. But now, the threads of that narrative had unraveled. The concept of authority had become a parody, and there was only a void in that absurdity.

He could hear footsteps approaching, soft, deliberate. His heart quickened, but it wasn't fear. It was awareness. Awareness of the moment when everything would shatter. He could hear the whispers outside the door, the rustle of fabric, the shifting of bodies. He knew they were coming for him. But there was no escape. He had no army left to command, no allies who would stand by his side. His wife, his cook, and the people who had served him were gone. They had already detached themselves from him, each in their own way. They had recognized the absurdity of his situation long before he had.

The door creaked open.

It was Elena again, but she didn't need to say anything. She didn't have to speak. Her eyes, cold and unwavering, told him everything he needed to know. She had come to deliver the final blow, though there was no violence in her step. No anger. Just the simple, brutal clarity of someone who understood what had to be done.

"The people are in the streets," she said, her voice low but firm, carrying a finality that left no room for argument. "It's over, sir."

"It's over," the words were not an accusation. They were a simple statement of fact. The people had chosen. They had decided to reclaim their lives and their world from the farce he had constructed. And they had done so not because they believed in a better leader, not because they sought some new figurehead. No, they had done so because they had realized, as he had, that the structure was hollow. Power was an illusion, and illusions could only persist as long as someone was willing to believe in them.

"I know," he murmured, though the words tasted like ash.

The garden of the presidency, vast and indifferent, was filled with the murmur of people gathering, a tide of bodies pushing forward, propelled by an anger that was no longer contained. It was not simply the people who arrived; they arrived with the army's complicity, a cold alliance forged in the hollow space between power and impotence. The soldiers, no longer the invisible protectors of the state, stood by the crowd as if they too had decided that the president, once a man, had become nothing more than a symbol of a dying order.

Inside the cold walls of the presidential palace, Elena's words reached him, sharp and final. "They're coming."

For all his grandeur and false certainties, the president felt the weight of his futility settle upon him like an iron cloak. His hands trembled as he picked up the phone, dialing the head of security. The man arrived quickly, but his steps were deliberate, his face resigned. It was as though he had already understood that his loyalty and obedience meant nothing now. When the president spoke, his orders fell flat, rebounded by the air of inevitability that had thickened around them.

"You don't understand," the president said, his voice wavering. "You must protect the presidency. You must—"

The head of security cut him off. "There is no point," he said, his tone void of emotion. "The country is angry. Your power is an illusion. There's nothing to protect. Resign. It is the only way."

The words rang in the president's ears but were already meaningless. He was, at last, naked in the face of the inevitable. The people were coming. Their steps were a slow, rhythmic march that echoed through the palace's corridors until denying them, or the situation's absurdity, was impossible. Once a towering figure, the president was now a man trapped within his skin, clutching at the remnants of a power he had never truly controlled.

They reached the gates. The sounds of their approach, the rustle of bodies, the chants, the growing crescendo of voices, told him all he needed to know. His back was pressed against the cold stone of the office, his mind racing for some way out. But there was no escape.

He stepped forward, fumbling for words, trying to explain, to justify his existence in the face of people who had already dismissed him. But their voices drowned him out, sharp and insistent.

"Resign!" they shouted. "Now, or we'll take you down ourselves!"

The president's body shook, and his legs felt weak. He opened his mouth to protest, but nothing was left to say. In the end, the decision was not his. The absurdity of his position became clear. The people no longer demanded an explanation; they demanded his surrender. And he had nothing left to give.

He stood there, trapped between the crowd's clamor and the crushing silence of his mind. In the absurdity of the moment, he saw himself reflected in their eyes, not as a man but as a symbol, one whose time had passed, whose presence had become an affront to the forces he had once commanded. He had lived too long in the illusion of his invulnerability, and now, this illusion had crumbled, piece by piece, under the weight of the collective will.

The crowd was at the gates now, their chants a relentless tide that washed over the once-sacred walls of the presidency. In a panic, the president sought to speak again, but words failed him. What could he say? That he had tried? That he had done his best? These words, so familiar in the corridors of power, now seemed like empty relics of a forgotten world. The people, these people, had seen through him. He was no longer a man with choices; he was a man who would be swept away, just as any other.

Standing at the door, his security chief had already decided. He did not offer reassurance or speak of loyalty. He stepped aside as though the protector's role had become irrelevant. "You must go," he said, flat and emotionless. "They'll be here any moment."

In the face of this disintegration, the president moved toward the door. His steps were mechanical, each one further distancing him from the power he had once believed was his birthright. He could hear the people so suffocatingly close that the walls seemed to bend under their weight. The air was thick with tension, palpable, as if everything in the universe had conspired to lead him here, to this moment of ultimate confrontation.

When the door opened, it was not the dignified entrance of a man who had made a decision but the hesitant, almost animal-like retreat of one who had been cornered. The people surged forward, their faces a blur of anger and demand. They no longer looked at him as a man but as a thing to be disposed of. They did not need explanations, and there was no need for a last speech. They wanted only his surrender.

"Resign!" they shouted again, their voices rising in unison, a chorus of contempt. "Now! Or we'll drag you out ourselves!"

The president stood at the threshold, a brief moment of absurd clarity flashing through his mind.

What was the meaning of it all? Was this the end of him? Or was it simply the end of a system that had never been anything more than a fragile illusion held together by the fear of the unknown?

Yani stepped forward, her voice barely rising above the raucous chants that filled the air, but somehow, in the chaos, her words cut through the noise. Her team, Ari, David, Estelle, Carlos, Christina, and Fael, stood ready, poised to intervene if things went south.

"You have every right to be angry!" Yani shouted, her voice steady but urgent. "But vengeance isn't justice! If we give in to that, we'll become the very thing we're trying to fight. Let the people decide. Let the system we've fought for take its course. We must rise above the moment, not drown in it."

A few crowd members hesitated, eyeing each other as if uncertain whether to agree or to continue the pursuit of immediate retribution. Yani's presence had a calming effect, but the fire in the crowd's hearts wasn't quickly extinguished.

A middle-aged woman, her face weathered by years of struggle, stepped forward, her voice cutting through the crowd's murmur. "She's right, but what about Elena? What about all the others who've betrayed us?" She gestured angrily toward the now-struggling president, who was being escorted away by the guards that had once sworn to protect him. "What about them? Are we supposed just to let them go free?"

Yani met her gaze; her expression was soft but firm. "No one is above the law. Elena will be held accountable. The system will work if we let it. But we can't sacrifice our values for vengeance. The people deserve a future where justice isn't about bloodshed but fairness."

For a moment, there was silence. Then Ari, Yani's boyfriend and team member, stepped forward beside Yani, offering a steady nod to the crowd.

"Yani speaks the truth," he said, his voice carrying a quiet authority. "This isn't about killing or arresting every person we despise. It's about building a new future, a real democracy where no one is above the law."

David and Fael stood nearby, watching the few who seemed more inclined toward violence and ready to step in if needed. The rest of Yani's team, Estelle, Carlos, and Christina, moved subtly to reassure the anxious faces in the crowd, letting their solidarity with Yani's message shine through.

Slowly, the tension began to ebb. One by one, the people seemed to remember the promise of something better. Their chants shifted from anger to unity, from calls for blood to the rhythm of hope.

"Yani! Yani! Yani!" The crowd's chant filled the streets, growing louder and more assertive.

The president, now safely outside the gates, seemed bewildered by the turn of events. He stood awkwardly, his suit askew and his face a mask of fear and disbelief. Elena, however, was still among the crowd, watching, her eyes cold and calculating.

Yani turned to her, her gaze meeting Elena's across the chaotic sea of people. For a moment, there was only silence between them, heavy with years of betrayal, promises unkept, and lost ideals.

"You've lost, Elena," Yani said softly but with conviction. "The people are awake now. You can't hide from that."

Elena's lips twitched, whether in disdain or something else, it was hard to tell. She straightened, her hand subtly signaling the guard near her to move her away from the crowd, but Yani knew this was over; the fight for the future had only just begun.

As the president was escorted further away, Yani stood tall, looking out at the people who had felt empowered for the first time in years. They had wrested control from those who had exploited them, and it was their moment, not his. Yet as the crowd began to disperse, she knew this fragile peace could shatter as quickly as it had been won.

"Let's get to work," she said, turning to her team. "The next fight, the election, is coming, and we must be ready."

The atmosphere in Yani's party headquarters was electric yet thick with the weight of a hard-fought victory. The walls were adorned with banners in blue and gold, the party's colors. People milled around in clusters: some nervously checking their phones, others speaking in hushed tones. There was a palpable energy that only came after a monumental struggle, after a dream was realized, after a movement became something more than just a slogan.

Yani stood near the back of the room, looking out through the expansive windows. The city sprawled out beneath the soft glow of the evening lights, and the streets were filled with people gathering, celebrating, and chanting. Her eyes scanned the crowd below, and her thoughts were a million miles away yet grounded in this moment.

Ari, always the first to step forward, came up beside her. He had a half-smile on his face, but his eyes told the real story. He was tired, exhausted even, but something in his expression reflected the triumph of what they had just achieved.

"We did it," he said softly, his voice a mix of awe and disbelief.

Yani exhaled deeply, glancing down at her phone. The final results were in. It was official: she had been elected president of the Republic. This was a victory not just for her but also for the people who had backed her, for the country that had dreamed of this day for so long.

Turning back to Ari, she nodded. "We did it. I'm the first woman president. But it's not over. The work starts now."

His voice was steady, but there was an underlying tension there. She had always known this victory would come with responsibility, a weight she couldn't afford to carry alone. Her party had not just won the presidency; they had swept through the legislative and local elections as well, securing majorities that would give them the mandate to change the very structure of the government. But that was the easy part. The real challenge lay in what came next.

Across the room, David, Estelle, Carlos, Christina, and Fael were gathered around a table, deep in conversation. Their faces were lit by the soft light of a dozen glowing laptops and phones. They had all been there from the beginning, fighting for a political victory and something that would last beyond one election cycle.

David looked up as Yani approached, a grin on his face. "It's happening, Yani. We've done it. The people have spoken. This country is ours, ours to shape. We're not just talking about change anymore. We're living it."

Yani's expression softened momentarily, but she didn't let the satisfaction last long. She could already feel the weight of the next steps. The promises she had made on the campaign trail, to bring transparency, rebuild the economy, and make the system accountable to the people, were now her responsibility. No more speeches. No more hopeful words.

"Yeah," Yani said, looking around at the team that had become more like family. "But now we have to deliver. People trusted us. And that's not something we can take lightly."

Ari, standing nearby, folded his arms, a more serious look replacing his earlier grin. "The people believed in us, but they won't wait forever. We need a plan. Fast. And it can't just be about passing laws. We need to show them that things are changing, that we mean it."

Yani nodded, acknowledging the gravity of his words. They had worked hard to reach this point, but now the hard part began. They couldn't afford to squander the momentum they had built.

"We've got the presidency, the legislature, and local governments," Yani said, looking at each team member. "But that doesn't mean we can take our time. We have to build from the ground up. The people are already out there, celebrating. But we can't let that excitement fade into disillusionment. We need to keep the pressure on and keep moving forward."

The End

ABOUT THE AUTHOR

Dwoeen Ngakié is a Gabonese writer whose work blends literature, law, and moral philosophy. A member of PEN America, PEN Canada, and the American Bar Association, his voice is shaped by postcolonial contradictions and a global perspective on justice. His writing combines legal insight with political depth and existential clarity.